WEAPON

THE STERLING
SUBMACHINE GUN

MATTHEW MOSS

Series Editor Martin Pegler
Illustrated by Adam Hook & Alan Gilliland

OSPREY PUBLISHING
Bloomsbury Publishing Plc
PO Box 883, Oxford, OX1 9PL, UK
1385 Broadway, 5th Floor, New York, NY 10018, USA
E-mail: info@ospreypublishing.com
www.ospreypublishing.com

OSPREY is a trademark of Osprey Publishing Ltd

First published in Great Britain in 2018

A catalogue record for this book is available from the British
Library.

ISBN: PB 9781472828088; eBook 9781472828095;
ePDF 9781472828101; XML 9781472828118

18 19 20 21 22   10 9 8 7 6 5 4 3 2 1

Index by Rob Munro
Typeset by PDQ Digital Media Solutions, Bungay, UK
Printed in China through World Print Ltd.

Osprey Publishing supports the Woodland Trust, the UK's leading
woodland conservation charity. Between 2014 and 2018 our
donations are being spent on its Centenary Woods project in the UK.

To find out more about our authors and books visit
www.ospreypublishing.com. Here you will find extracts, author
interviews, details of forthcoming events and the option to sign
up for our newsletter.

Editor's note

All images not otherwise credited are from the author's
collection. Imperial measurements are used in this book. For ease
of comparison please refer to the following conversion table:

1km = 0.62 miles
1m = 1.09yd / 3.28ft
1cm = 0.39in
1mm = 0.04in
1kg = 2.20lb / 35.27oz

Artist's note

Readers may care to note that the original paintings from which
the battlescene plates in this book were prepared are available for
private sale. All reproduction copyright whatsoever is retained by
the publishers. All enquiries should be addressed to:

Scorpio, 158 Mill Road, Hailsham, East Sussex BN27 2SH, UK
Email: scorpiopaintings@btinternet.com

The publishers regret that they can enter into no correspondence
upon this matter.

Dedication

To my parents for their unwavering support.

Acknowledgements

My thanks to the ever-helpful Jonathan Ferguson, Stuart Ivinson
and the staff of the Royal Armouries, Leeds. My thanks also to
the Light Weapons Wing, Defence Academy of the UK and the
Small Arms School Corps Infantry Weapons Collection Trust for
allowing me access to their wonderful collections. Thank you
especially to the individuals and institutions kind enough to
allow me to use their photographs to illustrate this book. I'd also
like to acknowledge all those who shared their experiences,
expertise and offered advice. Thank you to Nick Reynolds at
Osprey for guiding me through my first book. Finally, thank you
to my friends and family for their support while I got lost in the
history of the Sterling writing this book.

Front-cover images: (above) a Sterling L2A3 (© Royal Armouries
PR.9153); (below) troops of 1st Battalion, The Lancashire
Regiment (Prince of Wales's Volunteers) on patrol during the
Aden Emergency, 1967 (Express/Hulton Archive/Getty Images).
Title-page image: In 1958 the Canadian Army adopted a simpler
variant of the Sterling, designated the C1. It saw active service
with Canadian troops deployed with the UN peacekeeping force
in Cyprus between 1964 and 1993 as part of the force which
patrolled the Green Line buffer zone between Greek and Turkish
Cypriots. Here, a C1-armed Canadian soldier of Lord
Strathcona's Horse (Royal Canadians) stands guard as engineers
inspect a telephone line in Cyprus. (© Government of Canada.
Reproduced with the permission of Library and Archives Canada
(2017). Source: Library and Archives Canada/Department of
National Defence fonds/e010786821)

The Royal Armouries

The Royal Armouries is Britain's national museum of arms and
armour, and one of the most important museums of its type in
the world. Its origins lie in the Middle Ages, and at its core is the
celebrated collection originating in the nation's working arsenal,
assembled over many centuries at the Tower of London. In the
reign of Elizabeth I, selected items began to be arranged for
display to visitors, making the Royal Armouries heir to one of
the oldest deliberately created visitor attractions in the country.
The collection is now housed and displayed at three sites: the
White Tower at the Tower of London, a purpose-built museum in
Leeds, and Fort Nelson near Portsmouth. To find out more,
explore online at collections.royalarmouries.org

Imperial War Museums Collections

Many of the photos in this book come from the huge collections
of IWM (Imperial War Museums) which cover all aspects of
conflict involving Britain and the Commonwealth since the start
of the twentieth century. These rich resources are available online
to search, browse and buy at www.iwm.org.uk/collections. In
addition to Collections Online, you can visit the Visitor Rooms
where you can explore over 8 million photographs, thousands of
hours of moving images, the largest sound archive of its kind in
the world, thousands of diaries and letters written by people in
wartime, and a huge reference library. To make an appointment,
call (020) 7416 5320, or e-mail mail@iwm.org.uk
Imperial War Museums www.iwm.org.uk

CONTENTS

INTRODUCTION

The Sterling evolved significantly before it entered service. Here we see the first of the Patchett Mk I guns, serial number EXP.1 (left), next to an L2A2 (right). The Mk I uses parts, such as its barrel shroud, from the Lanchester submachine gun and feeds from a straight Sten magazine. In its final form the Sterling was a select-fire weapon which used a simple blowback action. To ensure reliable feeding the Sterling fed from a cleverly designed 34-round curved magazine; the magazine housing was also angled at 82 degrees to improve feeding. Built on a tube receiver with a perforated barrel jacket for cooling, the Sterling had a robust folding stock and was also capable of mounting a bayonet. To reach this final perfected form the design would go through more than a decade of refinements. (© Royal Armouries PR.9192 and PR.1413)

Since 1945, the British armed services have been engaged in over 70 conflicts in theatres all around the world, from Malaya to Aden and Northern Ireland to the Falklands. In many of these conflicts, at least until 1994, some British troops were equipped with perhaps one of the best post-war submachine guns: the Sterling.

Compared to the simple, cheap, but hastily made Sten submachine gun used by British and other forces during and after World War II, the Sterling was a work of art – part of a new wave of post-war submachine guns; utilitarian but refined, robust but cost-effective. While contemporaries such as the Swedish Carl Gustav m/45 and Israeli Uzi may be better known, the Sterling has an impressive combat history with countries all around the world, and remained in service with military and police forces across the globe for over 50 years. A British icon of the Cold War era, the Sterling may perhaps live longest in popular consciousness not as a weapon of war, but as the basis for the E-11 blaster rifle, the Imperial stormtroopers' weapon immortalized in the Star Wars films.

Before 1939 the submachine gun had been a niche weapon. With the exception of superior weapons such as the German MP 38 and Finnish Suomi, during the interwar years submachine guns were often expensive to manufacture, unusual in design or excessively heavy. Britain entered World War II without a submachine gun, however. During the war a generation of cheap, simple and quick-to-manufacture submachine guns emerged, including the British Sten, Soviet PPSh-41 and American M3, ideally suited to the war's industrial scale and the huge wastage of weapons experienced during the massive battles which came to characterize the conflict. The use of tube and sheet metal, stampings, pressings and simple welding meant that these weapons could be churned out in their millions. Even so, ergonomically and in terms of reliability and build quality, they left much to be desired.

The late-war Sten Mk V was an attempt to move away from the Sten's utilitarian roots by introducing a wooden stock and pistol grips as well as improved sights and a generally better quality of construction. While the Mk V served the British well in 1944–45 and later in Korea and Suez, the British Army was already well into the process of selecting its successor. Britain – unlike the United States and the Soviet Union, which moved away from submachine guns after World War II – saw the need for a small, portable but capable personal defence weapon to equip troops who did not need a full-sized rifle. The Sterling filled this niche for over 40 years, equipping rear-echelon support troops, aircraft and vehicle crews, medics, radiomen and officers.

With the cooling of relations between the Soviet Union and the Western Allies after 1945, it quickly became clear that the British Army rapidly needed to be prepared for another war in Europe. Accordingly, the early 1950s saw Britain embark on a rearmament programme. While a 'hot' war in Europe thankfully never materialized, a Cold War between the Eastern Bloc and NATO developed and British troops saw action around the world in a seemingly endless series of post-colonial policing actions in the Middle East, Africa and the Far East.

Despite being one of a class of weapons which was slowly being replaced by intermediate-calibre assault rifles – and competing against formidable contemporaries – the Sterling remained a successful commercial entity well into the late 1980s. While the Sterling was present at some of the pivotal battles of post-war British military history, it also armed military and law-enforcement personnel from many other countries including Ghana, India, Iraq, Kuwait, Libya, Malaya and Nigeria. In 1988, the end of production and the closure of the Sterling Armament Company signalled the loss of Britain's last large-scale, commercially successful small-arms manufacturer. Despite this, thousands of Sterling submachine guns continue to see service around the world – a testament to their quality and design.

ABOVE LEFT
A British Army 82mm mortar team in action during a summer exercise in West Germany; note their Sterlings close at hand. The L2A3 was frequently issued as the personal weapon of troops who primarily operated heavy weapons and equipment. (© IWM CT 1241)

ABOVE RIGHT
An Irish Guards section on patrol in West Germany, 1975. Most of the men are armed with the L1A1 rifle while the third man, a radio operator, carries a Sterling L2A3, commonly issued to radiomen due to the weight of the radio set. (© IWM CT 1223)

DEVELOPMENT
The origins of a Cold War British icon

ORIGINS

The Sterling Armament Company's most famous product, the Sterling submachine gun, may not have played a significant role in World War II, but the conflict was the impetus behind its design. Initially developed by George William Patchett at Sterling's Dagenham factory in Essex between 1942 and 1944, the Patchett would benefit from almost a decade of development before it was finally adopted by the British Army.

The firm began life in 1909, as the Sterling Telephone and Electric Company. Capitalizing on the emerging market for telephones, wireless radios and other electrical household goods such as vacuum cleaners, the company grew rapidly. By 1925, Sterling had built up an impressive manufacturing base, with its Dagenham factory covering 18 acres and having its own power station. Before the ascendency of Ford, Sterling was

The Sten submachine gun was developed in early 1941 and quickly entered production. The Sten Mk II, the most-produced variant, was the ideal weapon for desperate times, but after World War II it became clear that troops needed a better personal defence weapon. (Courtesy of Rock Island Auction Company)

Dagenham's largest employer. In the early 1930s, the company became known as Sterling Electrical Holdings Ltd and specialized in the manufacture of incandescent lights. Sterling's name changed again to the Sterling Machine Tool & Equipment Company in 1936. It was not until the outbreak of World War II in September 1939, that Sterling became an arms manufacturer, at first producing recoil assemblies for field guns before, in October 1940, being contracted to manufacture Britain's first indigenous submachine gun – the Lanchester. The company changed its name again in 1966, becoming known as the Sterling Armament Company Ltd.

The Lanchester

It is impossible to examine the development of the Sterling submachine gun without first briefly looking at the history of the Lanchester. The British military had been at best ambivalent, and at worst dismissive, about submachine guns since the end of World War I. An evaluation report dated 1919 from the British Army's School of Musketry on a captured German MP 18/I stated that pistol-calibre weapons would never replace the infantryman's rifle; such weapons would be issued only to those who could not carry a rifle, meaning the submachine gun was simply not required by the British Army (Helebrant 2016: 33). This attitude prevailed throughout the interwar period and as a result the British Army entered World War II without a submachine gun.

In June 1940, following the fall of France and the British Expeditionary Force's evacuation from Dunkirk, the British Army was in desperate need of small arms. Massive quantities of vehicles, equipment and weaponry had been left behind during the evacuation from France. All too late, the British military realized the need for submachine guns. In early 1940, the American M1928 Thompson submachine gun was adopted and the British Purchasing Commission in the United States ordered some 300,000 of them; but only 107,500 Thompsons had made it to Britain by December 1940, and it was soon realized that indigenous production in Britain was essential.

The Lanchester submachine gun was slow and expensive to manufacture, with a total of 75 individual parts including SMLE-style wooden furniture and a cast-brass magazine housing. The Mk 1*, with a simpler sight assembly and minus the fire-selector switch, was a limited attempt to simplify production. (Courtesy of Rock Island Auction Company)

George Lanchester worked to lighten the bulky Lanchester Mk 1, resulting in a series of three prototype 'Lightened Lanchesters'; here we see the second 'light model' with an unusual forward grip attached below the breech. (© Royal Armouries PR.7327)

In January 1940, Britain's Chief Inspector of Small Arms received for examination two German MP 28/II submachine guns from the British consulate in Addis Ababa, Ethiopia. The MP 28/II was a refinement of Hugo Schmeisser's MP 18/I, the world's first practical mass-produced submachine gun, which had seen action in the hands of German assault troops during World War I. In the interests of getting a weapon into production as soon as possible, the decision was taken in the summer of 1940 to build a British copy of the MP 28/II. On 19 October 1940, the Sterling company and George Herbert Lanchester, a technical advisor with a background in automobile and armoured-car design (having successfully developed the Lanchester 1927 armoured car which equipped the British Army's first mechanized regiments), who had been seconded to the company in 1939, were directed to produce a series of pilot guns at a cost of £3,615. Following the successful testing of the pilot guns the Ministry of Supply gave Sterling a contract for 50,000 submachine guns on 13 June 1941. The company was ordered to put the copy of the MP 28/II into production as quickly as possible. While Lanchester did not design the weapon which took his name, he oversaw its refinement for production and its manufacture at Sterling.

Of the 50,000 Lanchesters ordered, half were allotted to the Royal Navy and the other half were earmarked for the Royal Air Force to be used for airfield defence. By the time deliveries of the Lanchester Mk 1 began, however, the Royal Navy had been allotted the entire production run. While the Lanchester had in theory been adopted because it could be put into production rapidly, this turned out not to be the case. At peak production Sterling could only manage to produce 3,400 of the guns per month, despite having subcontractors manufacture a number of parts. Additionally, the Lanchester was time-consuming and relatively expensive to manufacture, costing £14 (£720 today) per gun. Sterling was awarded one final contract to produce Lanchesters in October 1943, with a total of 79,790 weapons being built by the end of production. Throughout the rest of the war Sterling continued to undertake other war work for the Ministry of Supply.

After he had completed his work getting the Lanchester into production, George Lanchester began an unsanctioned side-project. He turned his mind to improving and lightening the Lanchester Mk 1, producing a succession of three prototype 'Lightened Lanchesters'. These prototypes dispensed with the Lanchester's heavy wooden stock, barrel jacket and cast-brass magazine housing. Instead, the first two prototypes had Tufnol plastic pistol grips and bolted-on wooden foregrips. Although these prototypes were lighter than the 9.6lb Lanchester Mk 1, they were still significantly heavier than the Sten and Patchett weapons then in development. Interestingly, the third prototype, based upon the receiver of a Lanchester Mk 1, externally resembled the later Patchett submachine guns: the perforated barrel shroud returned and a new double-hinged folding stock was added; and the pistol grip, made from Paxolin, a sort of polymer-impregnated linen, was also moved slightly closer to the weapon's centre of gravity.

Although the Lightened Lanchesters were test-fired, the Ministry of Supply refused to consider them as they offered no significant advantage over the Stens then in service. While the Lanchester was a well-made, robust weapon capable of chambering the vast variety of 9×19mm ammunition available at the time, the fact was that it was based on an obsolete design dating back to the end of World War I. Despite this, the Lanchester outlasted the Sten in British service, and the Royal Navy did not declare them obsolete until 1978.

The last of George Lanchester's three experimental prototypes which attempted to lighten the Lanchester Mk 1, replacing the hefty wooden stock with a neat folding stock. This prototype bears more than a passing resemblance to Patchett's early prototypes. (© Royal Armouries PR.7328)

George Patchett and his machine carbine

It is unclear when George Patchett began developing his machine carbine, but he filed his first patent protecting the design in August 1942. This initial patent protected Patchett's trigger and fire-selector mechanism which removed the need for a tripping lever to actuate the sear to arrest the bolt when firing in semi-automatic mode. This was one of Patchett's first key improvements over earlier blowback submachine guns such as the Sten and Lanchester.

Two views of George Patchett's original toolroom prototype machine carbine, courtesy of the Small Arms School Corps Infantry Weapons Collection Trust. It was used extensively during early testing. Note the brazed-on sights and the folding stock added in early 1943.

In their authoritative work on the Sterling, Peter Laidler and David Howroyd note that Patchett's design certainly owed some of its most recognizable features to the Lanchester. These included the weapon's perforated barrel shroud that enabled air cooling, its magazine release and its front-sight protectors. The Lanchester's chamber design, which was capable of feeding almost any kind of 9×19mm ammunition, also influenced the later Sterling. Interestingly, both Patchett and Lanchester had backgrounds in the motor industry, Patchett having been a motorcycle racer and engineer during the 1920s, later working for both FN in Belgium and JAWA in Czechoslovakia. Lanchester was one of three brothers who owned and ran the highly regarded Lanchester Motor Company; HM King George VI favoured Lanchester limousines as his state cars. Sources suggest, however, that the two men did not get on and rarely if ever collaborated; and from 1942 onwards both were hard at work on their own submachine-gun projects at Sterling.

The first recorded test of a firing Patchett prototype took place on 25 September 1942, when Patchett demonstrated his weapon for the British Army's Ordnance Board, firing from the hip without a stock; a total of 412 rounds were fired during the demonstration and testing. The Ordnance Board reported that 'the carbine functioned satisfactorily', but disliked the prototype's lack of a stock and sights; they also noted concerns about the strength of the prototype's end cap (Ordnance Board Proceeding 19930, 12/10/42).

THE MAN BEHIND THE GUN: GEORGE PATCHETT

Before he turned his hand to small-arms design, George William Patchett was part of a pioneering generation of British motorcycle riders and engineers who pushed the capabilities of the relatively new technology. Information about Patchett's early life is limited; he was born in Nottingham and by the late 1920s had become a successful motorcycle racer for a number of manufacturers including Brough Superior and McEvoy. Patchett was an accomplished rider who pioneered the use of superchargers in short-distance time trials while at McEvoy. News of Patchett's record attempts, racing and record-setting regularly appeared in magazines such as *The Motor Cycle* and *Motor Cycling*. While he was often in contention, victory frequently proved elusive, but he did win the Welsh TT at Pendine Sands twice: first, in 1925, and again two years later, winning the Welsh TT's sidecar classification with a Brough Superior bike and sidecar. In October 1926, Patchett broke the short-distance speed record at Pendine Sands, reaching 85.35mph. The following month he took another average-speed record at the Brooklands motor circuit. For a short time he even held the motorcycle world speed record.

A talented engineer as well as rider, Patchett began to move into motorcycle design in the 1930s. For a time he worked for the Belgian small-arms and motorcycle manufacturer Fabrique Nationale (FN). It is believed that it was during his time at FN that Patchett first learned about firearms design and manufacture. In 1930, the Czech arms manufacturer František Janeček hired Patchett to design bikes for his new motorcycle company JAWA. Patchett developed a series of successful engine designs for JAWA during the 1930s which included 173cc and 248cc engines. Patchett also rode a JAWA motorcycle in the Isle of Man TT's senior race in 1932. In August 1936, he filed his first patent for a two-stroke engine.

With Hitler's annexation of the Sudetenland in 1938 and the increasing threat to Czechoslovakia, Patchett returned to Britain in 1939, bringing with him microfilm of his and Janeček's recent designs, including Janeček's anti-tank gun and projectile designs. Throughout World War II Patchett worked as a technical advisor and engineer at the Sterling Machine Tool & Equipment Company, where he initially worked under George Lanchester on the Lanchester submachine gun and other war work. (Reportedly, the two engineers did not get on and worked separately from 1942 onwards.) During this time, Patchett also helped to develop the De Lisle Commando Carbine's suppressor and a folding-stock prototype of the carbine. Leading his own design team, he began developing the Patchett Machine Carbine. In 1944, Patchett also patented a design for a power-driven machine gun and in 1949, a sled to help pull vacuum cleaners up stairs. He continued to work for Sterling into the 1960s and also designed the successful Sterling-Patchett Mk 5 suppressed submachine gun, adopted by the British Army as the L34A1. In 1957, Sterling and Patchett sued the British Government for patent infringement and for forcing an unfair production licence on the company. The government settled out of court, according to James Edmiston, Sterling's later owner, paying Sterling £228,000; the court ordered that half of this was to be given to Patchett himself. Adjusted for inflation, this settlement equalled roughly £4 million today (Edmiston 2011: 10).

In 1966, Patchett, together with the Ministry of Aviation – which at the time oversaw trade regulations – took Sterling to court over a design royalties dispute. In 1966, Patchett retired to Cannes, France; and the case with Sterling was settled a year later. He remained active well into his seventies and died in April 1978.

In early 1943, in response to the Ordnance Board's recommendations, Patchett developed a folding stock for his machine carbine and fitted the first rudimentary sights to the prototype – these were brazed on to the muzzle cap and the rear of the receiver. Patchett and Sterling filed a British patent protecting a 'collapsible butt' in May 1943. With a few later tweaks, this triangular design was extremely robust and locked securely. As with many firearms the Patchett went through dozens of iterations as its design was tweaked for reliability, ergonomics and manufacture. Early prototypes used the Sten's 32-round double-stack, single-feed magazine and leftover Lanchester barrels.

George Patchett's first prototype Mk I machine carbine, serial numbered EXP.1; the origins of the later Sterlings can clearly be seen in this early prototype. It has a lightweight folding stock and a simple peep sight, and feeds from a standard Sten magazine. (© Royal Armouries PR.7584)

One of the first production Patchett Mk I machine carbines, serial number 22, made for British testing during the later stages of World War II. Note the one-piece tube receiver, protected front sight and early plastic pistol grip. (© Royal Armouries PR.9140)

The Ordnance Board subjected the Patchett to its first real evaluation in March 1943, putting it through a series of sand, mud, heat and accuracy tests. Pitted against the Special Operation Executive's Welgun (developed by the Birmingham Small Arms Company), a Sten Mk II and a Lanchester Mk 1*, the Patchett struggled during the accuracy testing, failing to hit the target at 175yd. This is unsurprising considering the rudimentary nature of the prototype's sights. It fared well during the sand test, but failed the mud test. Even so, the Ordnance Board believed that the Patchett was 'capable of much improvement' (OB Proc. 22349, 26/03/43).

On 7 January 1944, the War Office issued a new specification for a series of new small arms including rifles, light machine guns, self-loading rifles, a medium machine gun and – most importantly for the purposes of this study – a machine carbine. This specification set out the required characteristics for a new submachine gun to equip the British military in the future. On 12 January, Sterling was contracted to manufacture 20 trials guns at a cost of £4,464, for further testing and evaluation. These weapons were delivered to the Ordnance Board on 28 April 1944. (The question of whether any of these saw action during World War II is explored later.) Sterling was not the only British company developing a weapon to meet the War Office's requirements, however. One of the oldest

names in British small-arms manufacture, the Birmingham Small Arms Company (BSA), also developed an impressive new machine carbine which would prove to be a worthy rival to George Patchett's design.

The Sterling's rivals

BSA had strong ties to British submachine-gun development as a major manufacturer of Stens during World War II, producing over 400,000; the firm also worked on its own designs, including a number of machine carbines for the Special Operations Executive. Designed to look like anything but a weapon, the Australian Andrews Machine Carbine, prototypes of which were built by BSA, was an unusual gun that was probably intended for covert work. The other, perhaps better-known submachine gun in which BSA had a stake was the Welgun, designed in 1942. While the Welgun never entered mass-production, it was used extensively during the machine-carbine tests as a comparison weapon.

In 1944, BSA began development of another new machine carbine, first tested in October 1945. Designed by Claude Perry, the BSA prototype employed the ubiquitous blowback action used by its contemporaries such as the Patchett and Sten, but had a number of interesting and innovative design features. These included a folding magazine housing which could be pivoted backwards to make the weapon more compact and allow jams to be cleared without having to remove the magazine. The BSA machine carbine's most distinctive feature was its cocking mechanism. Like the earlier Welgun the new weapon lacked a traditional cocking handle; instead, it was cocked by pushing the foregrip forward and then pulling it back. A rod connected to the grip pushed the bolt back and cocked the weapon; the user then rotated the grip to disengage the bar and allow the bolt to cycle once fired. This method of cocking shares some similarities with the BSA-manufactured BESA medium machine gun and the later prototype BESAL light machine gun.

In response to criticism of the Welgun's open receiver, BSA ensured that its new machine carbine was entirely enclosed, with only the magazine well and ejection port open when firing; when the bolt was closed these openings were covered, minimizing the chances of dirt entering the action. During initial testing the new weapon suffered failures and some of the test weapons were damaged. The BSA machine carbine was not tested again until June 1947 when the company submitted a refurbished and refined Mk II version which dispensed with the folding magazine housing and used a curved rather than straight magazine.

During an Ordnance Board test of the Patchett Mk II, BSA, MCEM3 and an Australian design in September 1947, the BSA was not put through 'adverse conditions' tests 'because of its present tendency to give misfires and cross-feeds under normal conditions' (OB Report Q5369, 28/10/47). By contrast, it was reported that the Patchett performed well. BSA again temporarily withdrew its weapon from the trial to improve the design. In March 1948, the improved Mk IIs were tested again at the Proof and Experimental Establishment (PEE) Pendine, Wales, where they performed very well against the Patchett and MCEM3. The BSA pulled ahead of

Patchett's design when the Ordnance Board reported that the Patchett 'failed badly in mud conditions and exceeded the [specified] rate of fire'; it was recommended that of the weapons tested, 'only the BSA is fit to go for troop trials', with the Ordnance Board recommending an order of 100 carbines (OB Report Q5545, 06/04/48).

It seems that by April 1948, the British military were so intent on adopting the BSA over the Patchett that Brigadier John Arthur Barlow – the Director of Artillery (Small Arms) and the man in charge of overseeing Britain's small-arms development – wrote to the military attaché of the British Joint Services Mission in Washington, DC. In his letter Barlow noted that 'we do not wish to be faced with a possible situation in which the US authorities … might adopt the Patchett, a weapon which is likely to be rejected by the British authorities' (Ref: 7/SA/25, 08/04/48, Barlow to Gosting at BJSM, Washington). In any event this call to dissuade the United States from testing the Patchett was unnecessary, as the Americans had dropped plans to adopt a new submachine gun.

George Patchett attempted to discover the cause of the problems suffered in the March 1948 trials and believed that the issue was with the ejector fouling the bolt as it travelled. Conversely, the Ordnance Board felt the problem actually lay with the Patchett's return spring not being strong enough. The Patchett was tested again in May 1948, and again suffered a large number of failures. Patchett had failed to address the correct problem and his changes to his machine carbine's ejector had no effect on the weapon's reliability. The Ordnance Board once again noted that it was the 'low weight of the return spring [that] was at least partially responsible for the malfunctioning'; the 6 August 1948 report recommending that no further action be taken with the Patchett (OB Report Q5721, 06/08/48).

The trials continue

George Patchett and the Sterling company luckily gained a reprieve when, in October 1949, the War Office issued a revised specification for a new machine carbine. It now called for sights graduated in 50yd increments up to 200yd, a rate of fire no higher than 500rd/min and the ability to mount a No. 5 Mk 1 rifle bayonet. Patchett continued to work on his design throughout 1950, eventually patenting a dual return-spring design with a

smaller spring inside a larger one. This increased the energy imparted to the bolt and addressed the Ordnance Board's earlier criticisms. The summer of 1950 saw BSA's guns tested under arctic conditions in Canada. The BSA was tested against a Sten Mk II and unsurprisingly was found to be superior in all respects.

During the late 1940s, as the Ordnance Board conducted testing of the new machine carbines, another small-arms programme was also under way, to replace Britain's venerable Lee-Enfield bolt-action rifles and to adopt a new rifle: the Infantry Personal Weapon. It was planned that this new rifle would replace both the Lee-Enfield in the rifle role and the Sten in the machine-carbine role, though arguably this new programme slowed the impetus for finding an immediate replacement for the Sten. Despite this, it was still recognized that a small number of rear-echelon troops would need an even more compact personal defence weapon. It was therefore proposed that the Danish Madsen M50 submachine gun could be adopted in relatively small numbers to equip these troops.

The Infantry Personal Weapon programme saw a series of rifles developed including two bullpup rifles and two conventional designs; one of the latter was from BSA, the other from the Belgian manufacturer Fabrique Nationale (this design would later become the FN FAL). All of these new experimental rifles chambered the new intermediate .280in (7mm) round. In March 1951, the British decided to adopt a bullpup rifle designed by Stefan Janson, the EM-2, as the Rifle No. 9 Mk 1. The No. 9 never entered service, however, as political developments saw the United States push for the NATO standardization of its new 7.62×51mm ammunition. The FN FAL was better suited to handling this new, more powerful cartridge, and so .280 and Janson's rifle were abandoned. In its place, in December 1953, the FN FAL was adopted by the British Army as the L1A1 self-loading rifle; but with the adoption of a full-power infantry rifle rather than the intermediate-calibre Rifle No. 9, the need for a dedicated submachine gun re-emerged.

The cost of setting up quantity production for a relatively small number of submachine guns had prevented BSA from fulfilling the Ordnance Board's recommended order for 100 new guns for troop trials. Instead, BSA submitted an additional six prototypes for further comparative testing. In November 1950, Sterling, perhaps aware of BSA's production issues, wrote to the secretary of the Ordnance Board to advise that the firm was 'now tooling up the Patchett machine carbine for quantity production, and shall be in a position in the New Year to offer

The EM-2 fired a smaller, intermediate-calibre cartridge, which made it more controllable than an automatic rifle. The British Army hoped that because of the new rifle's compact size it could replace both the Lee-Enfield rifle and the Sten submachine gun. The weapon shown here represents a later attempt to chamber the EM-2 for the larger 7.62×51mm round. (© Royal Armouries PR.880)

substantial deliveries of the weapons should they be required' (No. Q6767, Sterling to OB, 13/11/50). Sterling went on to note their history of arms production, reminding the Ordnance Board of their 'considerable experience over the last ten years in the manufacture of automatic weapons', namely the Lanchester (No. Q6767, Sterling to OB, 13/11/50).

Another round of trials at PEE Pendine was scheduled for January 1951. The Patchett Mk II was included as a control and for comparison purposes. Following the previous trial in July 1949, BSA spent 16 months attempting to refine its design based on the trials board's recommendations. Despite the company's efforts, however, an Ordnance Board report from October 1950 found that:

> The cocking mechanism also requires further re-design. It has been modified to require only 20 degrees turn for operation, but the shape has not been altered to restrain the firer's hand from going too far forward, and stripping and assembly are still difficult ... cocking became stiff in a hot weapon on several occasions, and two insert rotary sleeves fractured. Action is also required to avoid danger of firing a round accidentally while cocking, remarked on in the Canadian report. (OB Proc. No. Q6767, 12/01/51)

Indeed, the Ordnance Board recognized that a revision to the specification, made in October 1949, seriously affected the BSA machine carbine, noting that 'its cocking mechanism prevents the fitting of a bayonet which was previously only 'preferred' but is now essential. The necessary alteration to the method of cocking would be a major re-design, and trials of the new design would be required' (OB Proc. No. Q6767, 12/01/51). The report also noted that the BSA's trigger mechanism was overly complicated and needed to be simplified for easier disassembly. It was clear that a major redesign would be needed before troop trials could be carried out.

In January 1951, a round of endurance tests of the Patchett Mk II and Madsen M50 were ordered with each gun to fire 10,000 rounds. These tests were carried out by the Testing Section at the Royal Small Arms Factory (RSAF) Enfield and PEE Pendine in May 1951, with the Patchett and the Madsen being joined by the BSA Mk III and an Australian design, the MCEM-2 (not to be confused with RSAF Enfield's MCEM series of prototypes). The Australian design was not developed enough and performed poorly during testing. It was the BSA, however, which suffered the most during the testing. The Mk III was only able to fire 750 rounds during the endurance test before 'considerable wear' to the breech block and return springs was discovered and the test ended (Trial Report 51/47, 31/05/51). Additionally, the shape of the receiver near the ejection port was causing the breech block to strike the receiver as it travelled forward. This placed increased wear on the receiver and recoil springs. It was deemed that the BSA Mk III 'failed to pass the test since cocking by hand was extremely difficult' (Trial Report 51/47, 31/05/51). The Madsen M50 performed well and was found to require some small improvements and it was recommended that, due to sand- and mud-induced failures to feed, the magazine should be adapted to be double-stack with a double, rather

than single, feed (similar to the Patchett's) to aid performance. The report's only serious criticism of the Patchett Mk II was that its magazine lips needed to be reinforced. In general, it was said to have performed 'better than all other weapons tested' (Trial Report 51/47, 31/05/51).

The Patchett Mk II was able to fulfil the principal criteria of the War Office's machine-carbine specifications including a weight near 6lb, the ability to fit the No. 5 Mk 1 rifle bayonet, satisfactory reliability and disassembly without the use of tools. Conversely, the BSA Mk III required tools to disassemble its cocking mechanism, could not fit the No. 5 Mk 1 rifle bayonet, was slightly heavier and was not as accurate as the Patchett. Both weapons exceeded the 500rd/min criteria.

By mid-1951, the BSA Mk III was said to be nearly up to the standard of the Patchett Mk II except for its unusual cocking mechanism, which failed badly under certain conditions and had to be completely redesigned. At the same time, the Ordnance Board reported that the Patchett was now fully developed; the report noted 'its performance is excellent, being easily the best of all machine carbines tested in spite of a disadvantage due to hand-made magazines' (OB No. Q6975, 27/06/51). The Ordnance Board recommended the immediate adoption and introduction of the Patchett into service, noting that the Mk I had passed user trials successfully back in 1945.

Despite the Ordnance Board's recommendation, further trials were held in October 1951 to test modifications made to the BSA Mk III and Madsen M50. The BSA had been redesigned with an 'improved' cocking mechanism along with a heavily grooved grip and the ability to mount the No. 5 Mk 1 rifle bayonet; but the new cocking mechanism had the negative effect of increasing the weapon's weight by 10oz. The Madsen

The principal machine carbines tested by the British during 1950–52			
	Patchett Mk II	**BSA Mk II**	**Madsen M50**
Weight	6lb 3oz	6lb 4oz	6lb 5oz
Length (stock extended)	28in	27.9in	31.3in
Magazine capacity	34 rounds	32 rounds	32 rounds
Action	Blowback	Blowback	Blowback
Calibre	9×19mm	9×19mm	9×19mm
Rate of fire	578rd/min	551rd/min	615rd/min

Two views of the Patchett Mk I, courtesy of the Light Weapons Wing, Defence Academy of the UK. George Patchett improved his design incrementally as flaws were discovered. The Mk I evolved rapidly from his early prototypes: built on a single-piece tube receiver, it included a hand guard in front of the ejection port, protected front and rear sights and a refined stock. The Mk I still used the standard straight Sten magazine.

and the Patchett Mk II were both tested with new, improved magazines which improved their feed reliability. On 24 October, Sterling's director, Kenton Redgrave, wrote a terse letter to the Ministry of Supply questioning the need for yet further testing when the Patchett had passed all previous testing more than satisfactorily. Redgrave noted that on three separate occasions the Patchett had achieved testing scores of 99 per cent. Despite this, Sterling agreed to further testing from November 1951 into early 1952 (Redgrave to Ministry of Supply, 24/10/51).

During the endurance test, in which the guns each fired just under 10,000 rounds, the BSA suffered 46 stoppages while the Patchett suffered just six. The Madsen also performed poorly with 44 stoppages, largely due to failures to feed. The BSA suffered continued parts breakages and was withdrawn from the trial. Out of a maximum points score of 80, the BSA achieved 32.332; the Patchett was the clear winner with 78.224 (OB No. Q7207, 08/02/52). The Ordnance Board report concluded that the Patchett machine carbine was 'a fully developed weapon and the minor defects disclosed in the trial can be easily corrected' (OB No. Q7207, 08/02/52). In stark contrast, the Ordnance Board recommended no further action regarding the BSA machine carbine.

In October 1952, the Ministry of Supply requested 300 Patchett Mk IIs for troop trials. These were distributed to troops in theatres around the world including the Far East Land Forces and Middle East Land Forces commands, the British Army on the Rhine, and the British and Commonwealth forces in Korea. Others were sent to the School of Infantry at Warminster and the Royal Air Force, while other samples were also offered to Canada, the United States and Australia. The British Government's first substantial purchase from Sterling came in July 1953, with the purchase of 300 guns designated the 'Carbine, Machine, Patchett, 9mm, EX'. These guns were destined for troop trials. Further troop-trials Patchetts were purchased throughout the early 1950s and the weapons were extensively tested and universally well-received by soldiers and evaluating officers. One report, dating from May 1953 and compiled from evaluations from units on operations in East Africa, returned a raft of enthusiastic reports praising the Patchett. While all recommended the replacement of the Sten with the Patchett, the response from 4th Battalion, The King's African Rifles succinctly sums up the report's general opinion: 'it [the Patchett] has all the advantages and none of the disadvantages of the Sten' (Middle East Land Forces Report on Patchett Machine Carbine, 27/05/53).

A BSA Mk III with its stock folded and ejection port closed, courtesy of the Light Weapons Wing, Defence Academy of the UK. While the BSA's design is slick and ergonomic, its squarer pistol grip is not as comfortable as the Patchett's, although its folding stock is much quicker and easier to deploy.

A BSA Mk III with stock unfolded and cocking grip extended; note also the open ejection port. This weapon is in the collections of the Light Weapons Wing, Defence Academy of the UK.

THE PATCHETT MACHINE PISTOL

Alongside his machine carbine, George Patchett also developed a short, handy machine pistol. The Mk I Machine Pistol had an ingenious telescoping receiver with the rear section sliding inside the front section, reducing the length of the weapon by up to 4in. A locking lever just in front of the magazine housing allowed the telescoping receiver to be locked and unlocked. To ready the weapon to fire, the receiver was extended and locked in position; the bolt could then be pulled to the rear to cock the pistol.

The Machine Pistol incorporated a folding buttstock which pivoted up on top of the receiver rather than beneath it. The weapon also included a folding, spring-loaded bayonet designed and patented by Patchett. This folding bayonet was later tested on standard Patchett machine carbines and found to be insufficiently robust for field conditions. Despite this it rounds out what is an undeniably elegant machine-pistol design.

The Machine Pistol could be carried using Patchett's specially designed carrying rig, a belt adapter which attached to a soldier's webbing equipment and allowed an unloaded

Patchett to be carried at 90 degrees, ready to be brought into action quickly. Patchett's carrying equipment was never adopted, however; instead, the later Sterling was issued with a simple webbing sling.

One interesting feature that sets the Machine Pistol apart from all of Patchett's other designs is the order of the selector-switch settings. The standard order is 'S' (safe), 'R' (repetition), 'A' (automatic); due to a slightly different sear and lever configuration inside the Machine Pistol's fire control mechanism, however, the order is 'R', 'S', 'A'. No other Patchett-based design uses this configuration, and even the Machine Pistol's patent drawings show the standard selector order.

Patchett filed a patent for his Machine Pistol in June 1944, which was subsequently granted in 1948. The British Army's Ordnance Board tested the weapon late in the war, christening it the 'Carbinette'; however, as they had no specification or requirement for a machine pistol, the design was not taken up. Only a single example, marked 'Patchett Machine Pistol Mk I No. EXP.1', was built. Today, Patchett's Carbinette is held by the Royal Armouries.

Dubbed the 'Carbinette' by the British Army's Ordnance Board, Patchett's Machine Pistol had a unique telescoping receiver, a folding bayonet and a short over-folding stock. (© Royal Armouries PR.7590)

BRITAIN ADOPTS THE STERLING

Finally, in late 1954, following nearly a decade of development, refinement, testing, trials and incremental improvement, the British Army at last moved to adopt the Patchett machine carbine. The Ordnance Board reported that 'Its performance is excellent, being easily the best of all machine carbines tested' (OB No. Q6975, 27/06/51). The Patchett was designated the L2 and went through a final series of refinements during the mid-1950s.

In 1954, the British Army switched to an alphanumeric system of designations for small arms, with an 'L' prefix. The Patchett Mk II was designated the L2A1. At the same time, the British Army moved away from the term 'machine carbine', which it had used since 1940, and adopted the US term 'submachine gun'. The final incremental refinements made to the Patchett saw the British military's designations and Sterling's commercial nomenclature correspond. The refinements made for the military were also implemented in Sterling's commercial models. As a result, the later Patchett Mk IIs coincided with the L2A1; similarly, the Patchett Mk III was the same specification as the L2A2 and the finalized L2A3 coincided with the Mk 4.

The L2A1/Mk II, introduced in the summer of 1954, was the final weapon to carry Patchett's name, all subsequent guns being marked 'Sterling'. This coincided with Sterling's attempts to distance their product from its chief designer. In reply to a Ministry of Supply request to meet with Patchett, Kenton Redgrave, Sterling's managing director, replied that he 'strongly opposed the suggestion that Mr. Patchett should be called in to deal with any queries … our gun, recently adopted by H.M. Government was designed and developed by our company and technicians' (Redgrave to MoS, 01/07/54). Redgrave suggested other Sterling engineers were available, concluding that 'our weapon is the logical development of our previous weapon, the Lanchester Sub-Machine Gun, which was designed and developed by us before Mr. Patchett joined our organisation' (Redgrave to MoS, 01/07/54). This claim stretches the truth somewhat, and despite growing acrimony, which culminated in a court case, Patchett continued to work with Sterling for another decade. Finally, in August 1955, the Ministry of Supply requested a quotation for the supply of 15,000 L2A3s. Sterling quoted that each gun would cost £19 10s, equating to just under £500 today.

Refinements in service

Once troop trials were under way a series of refinements were made to the Patchett. The L2A1/Mk II was the first Patchett to incorporate an angled magazine housing which improved feeding reliability from the Patchett's patented curved, double-stack, double-feed magazine. The L2A1's light folding stock did not yet have the top reinforcing pieces introduced later, but did have a rib down the length of the stock to strengthen it. Another curved stamped-metal hand stop was also incorporated; identical to the

One of the early batch of L2A1s purchased for British Army troop trials, courtesy of the Small Arms School Corps Infantry Weapons Collection Trust. This gun, marked No. 06, has the short-lived small, weak front-sight protectors rather than the later, stronger stamped protector. Note also the reinforcing rib on the side of the stock, and the additional muzzle hand stop.

THE STERLING EXPOSED

9×19mm Sterling L2A3

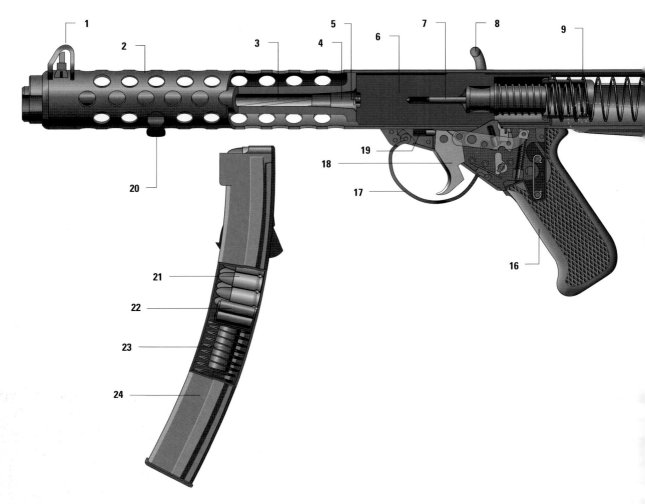

1. Front sight
2. Barrel sleeve
3. Barrel
4. Chamber
5. Firing pin
6. Breech block
7. Centre plunger
8. Cocking handle
9. Folding buttstock pivot
10. Back sight
11. Back-sight protector
12. Return spring cap
13. Sling swivel
14. Buttstock
15. Return spring cap locking lever
16. Pistol grip
17. Trigger guard
18. Trigger
19. Trigger spring
20. Bayonet lug
21. Cartridges
22. Magazine roller follower
23. Magazine spring
24. Magazine body
25. Chamber
26. Breech block
27. Centre plunger
28. Centre block
29. Inner return spring
30. Return spring cup
31. Outer return spring
32. Tripping lever upper arm
33. Cradle (shown semi-transparent)
34. Cradle spring
35. Location spring
36. Location spring retaining pin
37. Tripping lever
38. Change lever inner arm
39. Change lever spring
40. Sear plunger and spring
41. Sear

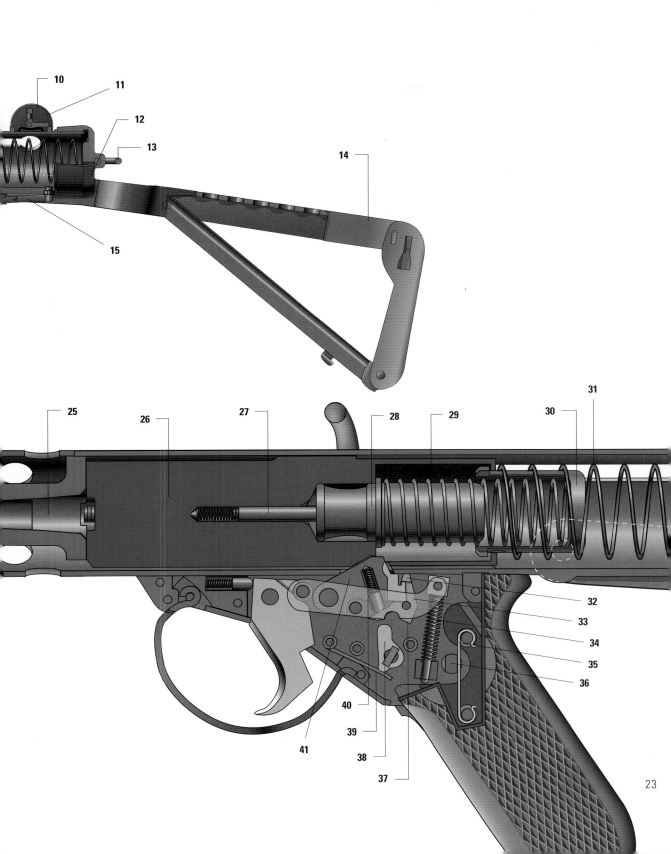

A close-up of the L2A1's rear-sight lever; this feature was present in both the L2A1 and L2A2 before it was abandoned for simplicity's sake. This weapon is held by the Small Arms School Corps Infantry Weapons Collection Trust.

piece in front of the ejection port, this was added just behind the muzzle on the right-hand side to prevent the user's left hand from slipping in front of the muzzle.

Sterling subcontracted the manufacture of the L2A1's plastic grips to Helix Plastics. The grips were made from Bakelite which proved to be too brittle for service conditions. The L2A1 also introduced the dual recoil springs devised by George Patchett to prevent light cartridge strikes. The L2A1/Mk II had a number of different styles of front-sight protectors, including some from the last remaining Lanchester stocks as well as stamped and folded sheet-metal protectors which would later become standard.

Introduced in February 1955, the L2A2/Mk III incorporated a raft of small changes which improved on the earlier L2A1. It was also the first gun to be marked 'Sterling' rather than 'Patchett' or simply 'GUN SUB-MACHINE 9MM'. The folding buttstock was strengthened with an additional top piece which ran half the length of the stock; this also provided a more ergonomic cheek weld. The cup between the two return springs was given a rim to retain the larger outer spring, the breech block was altered to simplify the cocking handle assembly and the end cap was secured with a small pin.

Both the L2A1 and L2A2 had a lever which flipped the rear sight from its 100yd to 200yd apertures. With the introduction of the L2A2 the diameter of the 100yd sight aperture was increased, as was the distance between the rear sight's protectors. Incorporated following feedback from

Introduced in 1955, the L2A2 was little more than a transitional model incorporating some small improvements to the design. Note that it retains the rear-sight lever, which was removed on the later L2A3. (© Royal Armouries PR.1413)

field trials, these changes allowed more light into the sight and enabled faster aiming. The L2A2/Mk III was little more than a transitional model and Sterling manufactured just 2,879 L2A2s for the British military and a further 1,570 Mk IIIs for commercial sale.

In September 1955, the British military formally adopted the L2A3, the version that would equip British troops for over 40 years; well over 500,000 military and commercial Sterling submachine guns would be made before production ceased in 1988. While the earlier L2 had been ordered in limited numbers for troop trials, the L2A3 was Britain's new standard-issue submachine gun, finally replacing the venerable Sten Mk II and Mk V. The first Sterlings began to reach British Army units in 1956, but substantial numbers were not available until 1957.

The L2A3/Mk 4 benefited from, and built upon, all of the improvements developed for the L2A2. For simplicity's sake, the L2A3

A Sterling-made Mk 4 with a No. 5 Mk 1 rifle bayonet, manufactured in 1974. (Courtesy of Rock Island Auction Company)

LIVERPUDLIAN STERLINGS

Although the Sterling had beaten all other contenders and finally become Britain's standard-issue submachine gun, the Sterling company's factory at Dagenham in Essex would eventually produce less than 15 per cent of the British Government's order of L2A3s. The Royal Ordnance Factory (ROF) at Fazakerley near Liverpool, which had produced Stens during World War II, had quietly been tooled up to produce the Sterling. This was a decision taken by the Ministry of Supply in the early 1950s.

In the late 1940s, the British Army recognized the growing Soviet threat to Western Europe. In 1947, Field Marshal Bernard Montgomery, the newly appointed Chief of the Imperial General Staff, wrote a paper outlining rearmament plans based on intelligence estimates of how quickly the Soviet Union was likely to be ready for another full-scale war. Montgomery believed that Britain had just ten years to develop new weapons and begin rearmament before the Soviet Union had recovered enough to launch an invasion of Western Europe. The British Army felt that rearmament needed to be complete by 1957; and in order to have the required number of L2A3s available, the production capacity of national arsenals

such as ROF Fazakerley would be needed. As such, the Ministry of Supply decided to have ROF Fazakerley produce under licence 90 per cent of the L2A3s needed.

In a programme codenamed *Pioneer*, the Ministry of Supply had the designs for the L2A3 redrawn for mass-production. The new plans were completed by August 1954, and the first ROF Fazakerley weapons, designated the X9E1, were assembled in the summer of 1955. Sterling was unaware of this decision and would later challenge the British Government in court, winning £228,000 in compensation in 1957.

Sterlings in British service were marked 'Gun, Sub-machine 9mm L2A3' or later 'Submachine Gun, 9mm, L2A3', followed by a serial number starting with either 'US' for Sterling or 'UF' for ROF Fazakerley production. The early Fazakerley guns suffered a number of manufacturing issues. They failed interchangeability tests with Sterling-made guns and 7,000 receivers were distorted by heat. ROF Fazakerley went on to produce the majority of the British military's L2A3s, 163,475 being made at the Liverpool factory, while Sterling produced just over 15,000 L2A3s. Production at ROF Fazakerley ceased in October 1959.

disposed of the rear-sight lever; the sight could simply be adjusted with the user's finger. The stamped front-sight protector was standardized, the front sight was simplified with a height-adjustable blade and an improved cartridge-case ejector was introduced internally. One major change to the L2A3 was a redesign of the Sterling's buttstock by engineers from the Ministry of Supply. The axis point was moved closer to the pistol grip and a full-length top strengthening piece was added, resulting in a very robust stock. The movement of the axis point closer to the grip also meant that the profile of the plastic pistol grip was altered slightly near the top.

THE SILENT STERLING

George Patchett first began work on a sound suppressor or silencer for his machine carbine in 1946. He developed a suppressor which could attach with relative ease to a standard Patchett Mk II. This was achieved by aligning the suppressor's side clamps with two factory-modified slots in the Mk II's perforated barrel jacket and clamping it in place. As Patchett's suppressor impeded aiming with the weapon's normal sights, each suppressor had its own set of sights, with a fixed sight at the rear of the tube and a folding front sight. While ingenious, the design was ill-fated. The suppressor was tested at the National Physics Laboratory in Teddington in May 1946 and proposed to the British Army's Ordnance Board in August, but the need for subsonic 9×19mm ammunition meant the project was given low priority and eventually abandoned. The design department at RSAF Enfield also attempted to develop an attachable suppressor for the L2A3 in the mid-1950s. This design also required specialist ammunition and did not progress.

As the Sten Mk II(S) and Mk VI had used standard 9×19mm ball ammunition, the Ministry of Defence sought a similar replacement for its ageing silenced submachine guns, issuing a requirement specification in November 1959. The new specification called for a 'silencer' that reduced the report of the weapon to the point that it was unrecognizable at 50yd. Alongside the engineer Bert List, George Patchett began work on developing an integrally suppressed version of the Sterling early in 1960. In June 1962, Patchett applied for a patent protecting his SV (Silenced Version), as he dubbed his design; the patent was granted in August 1964. The design owed much to the earlier De Lisle carbine, which Patchett himself had worked on, using some of the earlier weapon's leftover suppressor tube casings.

During field testing in October 1963, troops noted that in various environments the suppressed Patchett 'produced a lower noise level than the silenced Sten SMG [the Mk II(S)] and its silencing efficiency was not appreciably affected by use or wear up to about 2500 rounds'; the report also noted that 'mechanism noises [such as the weapon being cocked and cycling] from the weapon are limited … and were audible downwind to a maximum distance of about 50 yards' (OB Proc. 41391, 07/10/63). Field testing also revealed that the guns had a 'high incidence of short recoils indicating a tendency to runaway firing' when aimed up or down

(OB Proc. 41391, 07/10/63). To remedy this problem Patchett suggested the use of a lightened breech block, rather than the standard L2A3 block.

Limited production of the Sterling-Patchett Mk 5 suppressed submachine gun as the L34 was authorized in May 1965, and the Director General of Artillery approved the introduction of the 'Gun, Sub-Machine, 9mm L34A1' into service in January 1967.

As noted in Sterling's 1967 handbook for the L34A1, Patchett's suppressor worked by silencing the noise of discharge and also ensuring that the bullet left the muzzle at subsonic speed. To achieve this while using standard 9×19mm ammunition, 12 holes were drilled into each of the six rifling grooves, thereby equally spacing 72 holes along the length of the barrel. As the projectile moved along the barrel the fired cartridge's combustion gases bled off into the space inside the suppressor tube. This reduced the pressure behind the bullet and therefore reduced the projectile's energy, dropping the round's muzzle velocity to approximately 1,000ft/sec (below the speed of sound). As a result, standard-velocity service ammunition was rendered subsonic. The escaping gases were contained by the silencer casing, with some escaping through the holes in the front barrel support and others back into the barrel. With the column of gas having been largely broken up by the time the bullet emerged from the barrel, the gases were further dispersed by the spiral diffuser, with the interior shape of the front cap also contributing (Sterling 1974: 4).

Patchett's suppressor was impressively efficient. When his prototype, S.V.01 Exp., was tested by the Testing Section at RSAF Enfield in June and July 1960, the integral suppressor was found to reduce the Sterling's report to an average of just 86 decibels, compared to the 118 decibels of the unsuppressed L2A3 used as a control. The Testing Section reported just eight stoppages during the 5,572-round endurance trial and noted that the prototype suppressor completed the trial satisfactorily.

While the barrel length of the L34A1/Mk 5 is the same as the standard Sterling at 7.8in, its overall length is significantly greater at 33.7in with the stock extended. The suppressed Patchett is also substantially heavier, weighing 8lb unloaded compared to the L2A3's comparatively lightweight 6.5lb. The L34A1 and Mk 5 both have a different rear sight from that of

An early Patchett suppressed prototype developed in the mid-1950s. This design was significantly shorter than the later L34A1 and required the use of special subsonic ammunition, which prevented the design from being adopted. (© Royal Armouries PR.1434)

the L2A3/Mk 4: the first leaf has a normal single aperture, while the other is multi-holed with a circle of small apertures surrounding the central aperture. This gives a crosshair-like effect as well as a greater field of view and allows more light to reach the user's eye when aiming in low light. The apertures are also set higher in the leaves in order to compensate for the altered trajectory of the slower projectile. The suppressed Patchetts used the same front sight as the L2A3, although with a much-increased sight radius of 20.5in.

Sterling production of the Mk 5 offered two types of finish: a hard-baked black matte-finish Sunkorite paint over a phosphate-coated casing, or the more traditional Sterling black crackle paint. The British Army favoured the former for the L34A1, although a number of commercial Mk 5s were also purchased to increase Army stocks.

The testing at RSAF Enfield had reported that 'after firing one full magazine (34 rounds) it was uncomfortable to grip the weapon with the

bare hand as the outer tube became very hot' (RSAF Enfield Testing Report Silenced Patchett No. S.V.01, 22/03/60). In response, Sterling added a wooden foregrip to the Mk 5 commercial models, but no such grip was added to the British Army's L34A1s. Instead, field expediencies such as improvised canvas sleeves and woollen socks were used.

Unlike designs that relied on replaceable baffles which wore out, the L34A1/Mk 5 could be fired on full-automatic without much difficulty. This created more mechanical noise, however, as the gun's working parts cycled. To remedy this potential problem, a single-shot gun which fired from a closed, rather than an open, bolt was built. While the design proved the concept, it was not adopted or offered commercially.

As the L34A1 was designed for use by special-forces units such as the Royal Marine Commandos and the Special Boat Service, it was tested extensively by the Royal Marines in July and August 1961. They noted that the L34A1 had no traditional muzzle flash; instead, a 'small jet of rod

BELOW
This cutaway of a commercial Sterling-Patchett Mk 5 helps to show how the weapon's suppressor functions. The first section of the suppressor, where gas is bled off from the barrel into a mesh-filled section, can be seen, while ahead of that is a section of baffles placed in front of the barrel; this system reduces the speed of the bullet and the report of the weapon. Note also the weapon's lighter breech block and single, rather than dual, recoil spring at the rear of the receiver. (© Royal Armouries PR.9163)

While the L34A1 and the Sterling-Patchett Mk 5 are identical in design, the commercial variant (below) has an additional wooden foregrip and the classic Sterling black crackle paint finish. These weapons are in the collections of the Light Weapons Wing, Defence Academy of the UK.

sparks about a foot long' was noted, but these were reported not to be visible at distances greater than 40yd (Silenced L2A3 – User Trials, Infantry Training Centre, Royal Marines, 07/09/63). Concerns were raised about the 'continuous stream of smoke' which left the muzzle after firing; it was felt this 'would be very noticeable on a still, humid day'. The four test guns performed well, but one became so carbon fouled that after firing 500 rounds, the Royal Marine armourer wrenched away the front end of the suppressor, irreparably damaging it. A second gun suffered a similar problem and this was reported to Sterling as a potential flaw. The Royal Marines tested the perceived loudness of the L34A1 by firing the weapon over the heads of men who were lying behind cover, at various distances out to 100yd. They found that the sound the weapon made was 'acceptable if it is not repeated frequently'. It was noted that the 'metal to metal' noise made as the gun cycled was recognizably audible if one was familiar with the weapon. The report stressed that due to the subsonic speed of the projectile the weapon should not be expected to kill 'at a range greater than 75 yards' and that accurate shooting was essential for effective use (Silenced L2A3 – User Trials, Infantry Training Centre, Royal Marines, 07/09/63).

The Royal Marine Commandos were among the first to use the new suppressed guns in action. While operating in Aden, 45 Commando reported that the L34A1's end cap and catch became inoperable in gritty, sandy conditions. This had the effect of preventing the weapon's folding buttstock from being deployed properly. Interestingly, one of the first regular units to receive an L34A1 was the Royal Armoured Corps' Junior Leaders Regiment. The Junior Leader training regiments were made up of young soldiers who were training to become future warrant officers and non-commissioned officers for their chosen units. It seems likely that giving the new suppressed weapons to young soldiers would have ensured that they were rigorously tested by those most likely to break equipment.

Argentine commandos look over the kit captured from British forces at Government House during the invasion of the Falklands in 1982. Four of the commandos are armed with Sterlings including two Mk 4s, and the two men in the centre are armed with commercial suppressed Sterling-Patchett Mk 5s. The other weapons lying on the ground include L1A1 self-loading rifles, grenade launchers and Rifle No. 8 training weapons. (Rafael WOLLMANN/Gamma-Rapho via Getty Images)

The L34A1/Mk 5 was produced by Sterling under licence from George Patchett, who solely held the patents. When James Edmiston purchased Sterling in 1972, he also moved to buy the patents rights for the Mk 5 from Patchett himself – and agreed to retain the Sterling-Patchett name, much to the delight of the inventor. The British adoption of the Sterling-Patchett Mk 5 paved the way for sales to military and police forces in a dozen countries around the world until Sterling ceased trading in 1988. These included Argentina, Australia, Bahrain, Chile, Dubai, Jordan, Libya, the Philippines and Singapore. Sterling manufactured an estimated 3,500 Mk 5s, with the British military procuring as many as 500, although the latter number is unconfirmed. The L34A1 remained in service until it was replaced by the Heckler & Koch MP5SD, but some examples may remain in inventory.

NEW STERLING VENTURES

The Experimental Sterling S11

In 1965, in response to increasing pressure from competitors, Sterling developed a new prototype submachine gun. The S11 represented an effort to modernize production methods and compete with the Uzi and Heckler & Koch's new MP5.

Although George Patchett was still working with the company in 1965, the design of the S11 was overseen by Frank Waters, Sterling's chief designer, and David Howroyd, Sterling's engineering director. The S11 took a number of design cues from the Israeli Uzi. Unlike the original Sterling submachine gun, the S11 had a stamped rectangular, rather than tubular, receiver; and while the S11 took on an almost Uzi-like appearance it retained Sterling's standard curved, side-loading magazine. The S11 also moved the position of the charging handle from the right side to the top of the receiver and added a sliding dust cover to prevent the ingress of sand and dirt.

Sterling added a plastic foregrip, replacing the earlier weapon's perforated barrel jacket. The new foregrip allowed attachment of an L1A1 rifle bayonet, while the stock folded into a recess in the grip. The S11 moved away from the original Sterling's design with its barrel fixed in the receiver by a barrel nut similar to that used by the Uzi. Interestingly, the S11's sights were offset to the left to bring them in line with the user's eye. The box receiver necessitated a new stock design with two pivoting points either side; this appears to be a variation of George Lanchester's earlier folding stock used on his third 'Lightened Lanchester' prototype.

The S11 retained the Sterling's trigger and fire-selector mechanisms and a similar pistol grip profile. The new weapon had a new type of plastic grip, however, incorporating a prominent grip safety similar to that of the Uzi. The prototype was able to fit both the L1A1 rifle bayonet and the No. 5 Mk 1 rifle bayonet used by the Sterling. Whether this is a feature that Sterling would have retained for production models is unclear. The S11, like commercial-production Sterlings, was parkerized and given a black crackle paint finish.

The experimental S11 had a series of defects and interconnected problems including a loose top cover, feeding problems and trigger failures, none of which was unfixable. However, Sterling decided that rather than sink money into fixing the S11's defects and retooling for manufacture, it would be more cost-effective to retain the current design. Sterling produced a single prototype, serial number EXP 001, which the company later gave to the Ministry of Defence's Pattern Room in 1989. Today, the S11 prototype is held in the Royal Armouries' collection. Sterling gradually continued to lose market share as the Mk 4 was overtaken by more modern designs.

The Sterling rifle

Another interesting prototype developed by Sterling was a 7.62×51mm lever-delayed blowback rifle. The design was reputedly the work of designer A.J.R. 'Sandy' Cormack and Frank Waters. It used several components from the Sterling submachine gun, including the trigger assembly and pistol grip as well as a similar but elongated tube receiver. The weapon fed from either standard 20-round L1A1 magazines or 30-round L4 Bren magazines. Unlike Sterling's submachine gun, the rifle's magazine was loaded beneath the receiver rather than horizontally.

Neither of the existing prototype weapons, held in the National Firearms Collection, is complete and both are missing their butt assemblies. A reinforced receiver cap is evident on both prototypes, but a number of differences in the magazine housing, cocking handle and ejection port can be seen. The prototypes also differ in that one is configured as a light machine gun with a shorter barrel shroud and what appears to be a mounting point for a bipod. The light machine gun prototype fired from an open bolt and was locked at the moment of firing by a lever that locked on to the left side of the receiver. The rifle appears to have a slightly different action, with a different cocking handle, magazine housing and receiver extensions that house replaceable bearing surfaces for the delaying lever. The exact role of the Sterling rifles is also unclear; it may be that they were intended as a commercial offering or perhaps designed as a simple weapon for wartime production. The project was eventually abandoned and Sterling later went on to produce a licensed version of the ArmaLite AR-18.

One of the prototype 7.62×51mm lever-delayed blowback rifles reputedly developed by A.J.R. 'Sandy' Cormack and Frank Waters at the Sterling company. Using elements of the Sterling submachine gun's design including its pistol grip and tube receiver, a rifle and light machine gun were developed, but they never evolved beyond the prototype stage. (© Royal Armouries PR.7789)

COMMERCIAL MODELS

While the British military continued to use the L2A3, Sterling attempted to develop and market its submachine gun further with various other commercial designs which were adopted by a large number of foreign militaries and police forces.

Throughout the 1960s and 1970s, Sterling was eager to expand its product line and alongside the sale of licensed pistol, shotgun and rifle designs the firm also developed a series of weapons based on the classic Patchett design. A semi-automatic Police Carbine version of the Mk 4, which fired from an open bolt, had been introduced in the 1960s, and in the early 1970s, an effort was made to break into the US commercial market. Sterling's chief designer, Frank Waters, developed a semi-automatic Sterling, the Mk 6, which conformed to US regulations. In the British configuration with a 9.5in barrel, the Mk 6 looked almost identical to the standard Mk 4, except for a new Waters-designed barrel nut. For sale in the United States, however, the Mk 6 had a 16in barrel. Internally,

the Mk 6 had a heavier profile barrel and a new bolt designed by Frank Waters. The Mk 6 fired from a closed, rather than open, bolt and was semi-automatic only; it entered the market in 1972, but civilian sales were relatively slow.

In the early 1980s the Mk 4, Mk 5 and Mk 6 were joined by a new compact weapon, the Mk 7 Para Pistol. Essentially a Sterling Mk 4 with a 4in- or 8in-long barrel and no stock, the select-fire models also had a vertical front grip. Developed by David Howroyd, Sterling's engineering director, the Para Pistol was intended to be issued to vehicle crews and others who needed to store their personal weapon in restricted spaces. The Mk 7 came in both automatic ('A') and semi-automatic closed bolt ('C') variations. The A4/C4 weighed 5lb and was 14.75in long while the A8/C8 weighed 5lb 4oz and measured 18.5in overall. Both of these models could be fitted with optional plastic buttstocks and 'scope rails for tactical applications. The Para Pistol retailed for £180 during the 1980s, but Peter Laidler estimates that just 300 automatic Mk 7s and 900 closed-

One of the Sterling Armament Company's last commercial offerings, a semi-automatic Mk 8 with a fixed plastic buttstock and an optic-mounting rail to improve accuracy. (© Royal Armouries PR.9188)

At just 15in long, the Mk 7 A4 Para Pistol was Sterling's most compact submachine gun. This weapon is in the collections of the Light Weapons Wing, Defence Academy of the UK.

bolt Mk 7s were sold before production ceased in 1988 (Laidler & Howroyd 1996: 231).

Sterling's final commercial offering, the Mk 8, was introduced in late 1983. Differing little from the earlier Mk 6, the closed-bolt, semi-automatic Mk 8 simply had a different barrel attachment system and could fix a bayonet like the Mk 4. According to a Sterling brochure, the Mk 8 was designed to offer superior accuracy at ranges of 100–200m (109–219yd), presumably for situations where innocent members of the public were present. This was no doubt a sales pitch developed in the context of recent high-profile terrorist attacks such as the Iranian Embassy Siege in London in May 1980. Fewer than 100 Mk 8s were produced before the Sterling Armament Company closed down in 1988.

Made by Sterling in the early 1970s for a Saudi Arabian customer, this gold-plated presentation-model Mk 4 is complete with golden magazine, bayonet and cleaning kit, and a leather carrying case. Sterling produced at least 25 chrome-plated and 20 24kt gold-plated Mk 4s. These presentation guns were predominantly sold to customers in Middle Eastern countries including Iraq, Kuwait, Qatar and Saudi Arabia. (© Royal Armouries PR.9695)

USE
Patchett's gun in action

INTO SERVICE

After years of development, testing and evaluation the British Army officially adopted George Patchett's submachine gun in September 1953. The subsequent major contract for improved L2A3s was signed in September 1955. The British armed forces did not begin to receive deliveries of the L2A3 until 1957, however. This was in part due to the Ministry of Defence's policy to allow overseas orders to be fulfilled first to quality-test the tooling and weapons manufactured. Despite this policy, by the late 1950s British troops on operations around the world were equipped with the L2A3, which would remain in active service into the 1990s.

In British service, the Sterling was designated the 'Submachine Gun, 9mm, L2A3', but to generations of British troops it was simply known as the SMG. The Sterling was potentially the personal defence weapon issued to anyone who had a primary task that was not firing a rifle or a general-purpose machine gun. It was issued to a wide range of personnel, including medics, radio operators, anti-tank weapon crews, dog handlers, military police, mortar sections, lorry drivers and engineers. The Sterling L2A3 was the standard personal defence weapon for all armoured-vehicle crews of the Royal Armoured Corps. Almost all of the British Army's armoured vehicles were fitted with racks to store the crews' personal weapons, unloaded, until needed.

The British Army's revised 1977 manual for the L2A3 stated that the weapon could be fired from the waist or the shoulder. Its effective range was 75m (82yd) when engaging fleeting targets; while this range could be increased when engaging stationary targets with aimed fire, the drop-off in penetration meant that 150m (165yd) was a practical limit to the weapon's effective range (Sterling Sub-Machine Gun, User Handbook, 9mm MK4/L2A3).

DID THE PATCHETT SEE ACTION DURING WORLD WAR II?

One of the most enduring mysteries surrounding the Sterling is when exactly it first saw action. It has been suggested that a number of Patchett machine carbines were issued to British paratroopers of 1st Airborne Division during Operation *Market Garden* in September 1944. Despite much research, however, there is currently no documentary evidence to suggest that trials Patchetts found their way to the legendary battle that consumed Arnhem. Four Patchetts were sent to the Airborne Forces Development Centre (AFDC) in April 1944 (the AFDC was tasked with testing and developing applications for equipment intended for issue to British paratroopers and glider infantry) to evaluate how well suited they were for use by airborne troops. Laidler and Howroyd hypothesize that the three trials guns which were not returned after the end of the AFDC's testing in January 1945, Patchetts with serial numbers 067, 070 and 072, may have found their way to Arnhem. This is based on circumstantial evidence at best, however. While early Sten Mk Vs were issued to elements of the airborne landing troops who preceded the D-Day landings in June 1944, with photographic evidence supporting this, there is no evidence that the same was done with the Patchett during Operation *Market Garden*.

The Imperial War Museum's collection includes a Patchett Mk I machine carbine with the serial number 078. This weapon was handed in to police during a Home Office firearms amnesty with the accompanying information suggesting that it had been carried by Lieutenant-Colonel Robert Dawson, commanding officer No. 4 Commando. Dawson is said to have carried No. 078 as part of field trials during Operation *Infatuate*, the Allied landings to capture the occupied Dutch island of Walcheren, on 1–8 November 1944. The serial number 078 is outside of the first 20 trials weapons ordered on 12 January 1944. These weapons' serial numbers ran from 053 to 073, with a second batch of 100 Patchetts ordered in June 1944. This second batch ran from serial number 080 to 180 – which raises the question: what was the fate of the five guns marked 074 to 079? These were not funded by a government contract. Sadly, many of the Sterling company's records were destroyed by fire on 21 March 1945, when a V-1 flying bomb destroyed the offices holding the company's registers. I have been unable to find any record of a trials gun being issued to No. 4 Commando.

Another documentary indication that the Patchett saw active service during World War II comes from the introduction of an Ordnance Board report from January 1951. It discusses how the Patchett 'had been used in action by Combined Operations troops [better known as the Commandos]' and had been recommended as a replacement for the Sten in January 1945 (OB Investigation No. 1767, Machine Carbines, 12/01/51).

There is also a tantalizing photograph of a group of men who are believed to be members of the Free French 3rd SAS Regiment operating in the northern Netherlands, possibly during Operation *Amherst* on 7–8 April 1945. The somewhat grainy photograph shows a group of men wearing Denison smocks and armed with an M1928 Thompson submachine gun, a perennial favourite of Allied commandos, and two unmistakable Patchett machine carbines. While the photograph is grainy, the profile of the Patchett's sweeping grip and folding stock is clear to make out. Sadly, this photograph also lacks the provenance to confirm the suggestion that the Patchett saw action with commandos during the war.

The claim that the Patchett was used during World War II is also noted in one of the early handbooks written by George Patchett to accompany his weapon. Published in May 1948, it states that British commando units used the gun following extensive testing. This could certainly be a reference to one of the possible uses previously discussed, but the mystery as to whether the Patchett saw action during World War II persists.

Korea

During the testing and development of the Patchett, the British Army subjected the new machine carbines to troop trials in a number of theatres including Korea, Kenya and Malaya before adoption. A total of 116 Patchett machine carbines were sent to British and Commonwealth troops in Korea for field testing. Maynard Leslie Winspear served as an NCO with the Intelligence Section of 1st Battalion, The Duke of Wellington's Regiment (West Riding) during the Korean War (1950–53). While serving in Korea in 1952–53, Winspear's battalion was one of the units selected to test and evaluate the Patchett in the field. Winspear was impressed by the Patchett's accuracy:

we were asked to test it, I took it out with me and went up the valley next to where the headquarters was and there was an outcrop of rock on a cliff about 300 yards away ... and I fired 28 rounds out the magazine, it was a curved magazine, and every shot pinged off this [outcrop]. The Sten barrel was about four inches long after the chamber, this [the Patchett] was about six inches and it was incredibly accurate, more accurate than it needed to be. (IWM 32589)

Another soldier then buried the new submachine gun 'by a stream in the sand, the waterlogged sand'; Winspear recalled that the soldier returned a couple of days later, 'pulled it out, cleaned it with his fingers, blew down the barrel, put a round in the chamber and fired it and it functioned perfectly' (IWM 32589). Winspear felt that the lighter weight of the Patchett's 9×19mm round meant he could carry much more ammunition than a rifleman: 'I used to carry 100 rounds, 50 in the bandolier in the front and 50 in the back and each bandolier weighed about a kilo [2.2lb], if you had 100 rounds on you, you could last a long time' (IWM 32589).

Robert Hawksworth of 1st Battalion, The Durham Light Infantry, also tested the Patchett in Korea. He was ordered to put it through rigorous testing:

The Patchett we took with us to Korea on troop testing ... with instructions to give it a bashing, use it and put it through the most rigorous tests and report in due course. But on no accounts, was it to be taken through the wire, we didn't want the [Communist North Korean/Chinese forces] to get hold of these weapons at that time. I had one personally and gave it a fill of testing, including a total immersion in a frozen well for 24 hours and within a matter of minutes of recovery [it was] firing effectively. (IWM 12708)

In May 1953, Australian troops of The Royal Australian Regiment, part of the Commonwealth Division, also tested the Patchett. The Chief of the

TRAINING

Training with the Sterling began in the classroom, where new soldiers were taught how to handle, disassemble and clean the weapon before being taken to the firing range. In 1955, the War Office issued 'Infantry Platoon Weapons Pamphlet No. 4' which outlined how instructors were to train troops to use the new submachine gun over the course of three classroom lessons. The first lesson covered the assembly, disassembly and cleaning of the weapon; the second lesson covered loading, unloading, firing and immediate-action drills; while the third lesson covered how the weapon worked and what stoppages might be encountered and how to remedy them. Troops were then tested on magazine loading and unloading, weapons handling, manipulation and field stripping. The tests were marked out of 50, with those achieving 45–50 being graded 'skilled', while those who scored only 25 or less failed. A recruit was expected to achieve at least an 'average' grade, while trained men with weapons-handling experience who could not achieve 'above average' or 'skilled' were deemed to require more instruction.

Following these lessons and training tests, the troops would then be allowed to fire the weapon at the firing range. Instructors would lead the students through 11 'practices' of firing in semi-automatic and fully automatic at ranges between 5yd and 75yd. The first five practices saw troops fire five rounds at various ranges from both the shoulder and the hip. The sixth and seventh practices had troops engage targets from the hip at close range (10yd). The final four practices had troops engage targets at 35yd and 75yd, firing from the shoulder for accuracy. From this course of fire, using two magazines of ammunition, it is clear that the emphasis was on aimed, deliberate, semi-automatic fire at ranges of 15–75yd. The training pamphlet advised instructors to emphasize that while it was possible to shoot from the waist in an emergency or at point-blank range, it was always better to fire from the shoulder.

Lance Corporal Bill Carter of the Royal Military Police, who were predominantly trained and issued with the Sterling and the Browning L9A1 automatic pistol, remembered his training in the early 1960s: 'we were shown the weapon in the classroom first, how to take it apart, how to clean it … once the firearms instructor thought you were capable of what came next, the firing and loading, they took you down the range' (IWM 27245). Instructors were to repeat the course of fire with students as time and ammunition allowed. A soldier was not considered fully trained until he had completed a course of fire on a field training range under simulated battle conditions where he had to engage fleeting and mobile targets from a variety of positions. Once qualified with the Sterling, troops were awarded skill-at-arms badges; the SMG Marksman badge consisted of the letters 'SMG' inside a wreath, and was worn on the left forearm.

In April 1973 the British Army formalized the pattern for a specially adapted 'drill purpose' Sterling, taking worn-out L2A3s and converting them into L49A1 inert training weapons. The L49A1, developed for squad drill training purposes, still loaded and functioned with drill rounds and disassembled just like a normal L2A3. To fabricate an L49A1, parts from unserviceable L2A3s were used where possible. The breech block was scalloped, several cuts were made to the perforated barrel casing and the barrel was welded into the receiver casing. Existing markings on the magazine housing were crossed out and replaced with 'L49A1 DP'. A white band was painted around the receiver just above the pistol grip with 'DP' painted in black on both sides. The end cap was also painted white and 'DP' added. (© Royal Armouries PR.7594)

Australian General Staff, Lieutenant General Sir Sydney Rowell, was also shown the new weapon during a visit to Australian units in Korea. In September 1954, the Australian Army completed its own testing and evaluation of the Patchett that included climate and mud tests, as well as

endurance and accuracy testing. A Mk 2/3 Owen Gun was used as a control for comparison purposes. While the Owen, with its longer barrel, performed slightly better in accuracy testing, the Patchett's overall performance was considered better. The report concluded by recommending the adoption of the Patchett for Australian service; but though the Australians were impressed by the Patchett they did not follow this recommendation. Instead, they later adopted the indigenously developed F1 submachine gun which borrowed some features from George Patchett's design, including its magazine.

Canadian troops from 25th Canadian Infantry Brigade also tested the Patchett in Korea. In June 1953, George Maguire, a senior armourer with 25th Canadian Infantry Brigade, told the *Ottawa Citizen* newspaper that 'at 30 yards it can fire 2 ½-inch groups, which is as good as a service rifle can do.' He continued, 'I've been riddling tin cans regularly with it at 150 yards. The effective range for most nine-millimetres is 125 yards' (quoted in *Ottawa Citizen*, 15/06/53). Brigadier Jean Allard, the commander of 25th Canadian Infantry Brigade, endorsed recommendations for the Patchett to be issued for use by Canadian troops fighting in Korea. Canadian troops would not receive the new submachine guns until after production of the C1 began in 1959, however.

This Patchett Mk II, serial number 2772, is in the collections of the Light Weapons Wing, Defence Academy of the UK. It was one of several trials guns which had a shotgun-style rib sight fitted along the length of the receiver to aid snap shooting in the jungle.

The Malayan Emergency

Between 1948 and 1960 British troops were engaged in counter-insurgency operations against Communist guerrillas in Malaya. This offered an arduous theatre of operations for field testing of the new Patchett. By late 1953, just under 550 Patchett Mk IIs had been sent to the British Army's Far East Command where they saw extensive testing. The Patchett

Malaya, 1958 (overleaf)

A British patrol stumbles into the enemy deep in the Malayan jungle. A small patrol of the communist insurgent Malayan National Liberation Army (MNLA) equipped with double-barrelled shotguns and captured Lee-Enfield bolt-action rifles opens fire, but the better-armed British troops quickly gain fire superiority. The British point man opens fire at close range with his newly issued Sterling, killing an MNLA officer armed with a Sten Mk II. In the background the rest of the patrol – armed with an L1A1 self-loading rifle, an Australian Owen Gun, favoured for its reliability by Commonwealth troops operating in Malaya, and a Bren gun – exchange fire with the MNLA troops, driving them back.

performed well during troop trials carried out during the Malayan Emergency. During the field trials an interesting modification was made to at least three Patchetts in an effort to improve 'first shot hit' probability. The modification saw the removal of the standard fore and back sights and the fitting of a shotgun-style rib sight which ran the length of the weapon. During operations in Malaya and Borneo, many scouts and point men often carried shotguns like the semi-automatic Browning Auto-5. Shotguns were a favoured weapon during jungle operations because of the ease with which they could be aimed quickly and instinctively, and their exceptional close-range firepower. This battlefield modification to the Malayan trials Patchetts was intended to enable users to engage fleeting targets in thick jungle and heavy rainstorms. The modifications were short-lived, however, and later Patchetts were provided with wider rear-sight apertures.

Kenya

In October 1952, a state of emergency was declared in the British East African colony of Kenya after a group known as the Mau Mau began an insurgent uprising against British rule, targeting white settlers and any Kenyans who did not support them. The Kenyan authorities and the British Army fought a three-year counter-insurgency campaign to quell the rebellion.

The Kenya Police were an early adopter of the Patchett, purchasing 550 Mk II weapons from Sterling. In early 1955, a patrol from the Murengeti police post broke up a Mau Mau ambush that had seriously wounded a Kenyan Home Guard member. The Mau Mau stole the man's rifle and fled, only to be cornered in an area of forest. The Kenya Police set up a cordon and an officer entered the bush and sprayed the undergrowth with his Patchett. The Mau Mau immediately broke cover and were cut down by the police cordon.

Kenya was another of the theatres of operations to which trials guns were sent for field testing; 200 Patchetts were sent to units in East Africa for evaluation. 1st Battalion, The Black Watch (Royal Highland Regiment) was one of the units to receive the Patchett Mk II for field testing in Kenya. At least one Patchett was used during the ten-hour-long Christmas Eve Battle, during which a large band of Mau Mau were surrounded in a copse near Thaika on 24 December 1953. As the soldiers and policemen closed in, a fierce exchange of fire began; it was not until the next morning that the battle ended, with five Mau Mau dead and four wounded (van der Bijl 2017).

While the Patchetts and later Sterlings used in Kenya suffered few problems, some of the ammunition issued for use in them left much to be desired. In October 1957, while hunting for the Mau Mau leader Dedan Kimathi, a native Kenya Police officer was bandaging his injured foot when Kimathi crossed a clearing in front of him. The officer grabbed his Patchett and squeezed the trigger – nothing. The poor-quality ammunition issued to the Kenya Police failed to fire and the Mau Mau leader escaped. Derek Franklin, a member of the Kenya Police's Special Branch during the

1950s, also recalled problems with the age of the available ammunition, but when offered the choice between a Sten and a Sterling he decided on the latter, praising its superior accuracy and firepower (Franklin 1997: 127). While serving in Kenya, Franklin made extensive use of his Sterling. During an attack on a Shifta (bandit) camp he was challenged at a range of only 10yd and opened fire,

Two Kikuyu tribesmen working with a patrol tracking Mau Mau insurgents. The man on the left is armed with an L1A1 self-loading rifle while the man on the right has a Patchett Mk II, possibly one of the early batch bought by the Kenya Police. (© IWM MAU 685)

discharging almost a full magazine; this was the signal for the rest of his party to start shooting (Franklin 1997: 4). During another operation, patrolling along the eastern bank of the Uaso Nyiro River, Franklin and his men encountered a Mau Mau group which immediately fled, jumping into the river to hide. Franklin spotted a hat floating among some reeds and waded into the river to investigate. Carrying his Sterling over his head he reached out for the hat, and was startled when a Mau Mau leapt up and attacked him with a machete. Although Franklin recalled very little about the moments that followed, he and his patrol accounted for two Mau Mau armed with *pangas* (large cutting tools) and homemade guns (Franklin 1997: 47). Franklin's experience shows just how well the Sterling performed in the difficult conditions in which it was deployed. Even submerged in water it still functioned flawlessly.

Peter Hewitt, another police officer serving during the Mau Mau Uprising, firmly believed that the Sterling was the ideal weapon to provide rapid, accurate fire at the beginning of a firefight (Hewitt 2008: 242). Compared with the Lee-Enfield bolt-action rifles with which Hewitt's men were armed, the Sterling provided the kind of firepower which was essential in short, fast-paced, close-quarter engagements. During one patrol, Hewitt and his men were led to an insurgent camp by a former Mau Mau. Creeping into the camp early in the morning, they were spotted, and Hewitt opened fire on two fleeing targets. One of the bursts from his Sterling caught one of the fugitives, sending him tumbling to the ground (Hewitt 2008: 239).

An official report correlating many of the evaluations returned by units in the field included several from units serving in Kenya. The reporting officer for 7th Battalion, The King's African Rifles praised the Patchett in glowing terms, believing it to be ideal for combat at close quarters (Middle East Land Forces Report on Trials of the Patchett Machine Carbine, 27/05/1953). The British counter-insurgency campaign and disunity among the Mau Mau led to the collapse of the armed Mau Mau Uprising and remaining support within the general population ebbed away by 1958.

MAGAZINES

In May 1946, George Patchett patented a new curved magazine that would become one of the Sterling's most recognizable features. Initially, the Sterling had been designed to use the standard Sten magazine. Arguably, this was the Sten's weakest feature – the double-stack, single-feed 32-round magazine was difficult to load and fed unreliably. Patchett addressed this by giving his magazine a curve, allowing the slightly tapered 9×19mm rounds to feed more reliably. He also replaced the traditional magazine follower with a pair of rollers which minimized friction and allowed dust, grit and dirt to be rolled out of the way, thus improving reliability. Patchett's magazine was designed so it could be economically stamped from sheet metal and folded and spot-welded into shape. It was simple to disassemble for cleaning and required no tools. In 1952, Patchett added a pair of strengthening ribs to the inside of the magazine which also further reduced friction on the rollers. He also replaced the oval follower spring with a more efficient circular one with the ribs acting to hold it in place. The Sterling's magazine was substantially easier to load and could hold 34 rounds.

The magazines used by the British military differed from Patchett's design. The British Government, perhaps unwilling to purchase the rights to manufacture Patchett's design, developed the 'Magazine, L1A2'. Nearly 2 million of these were produced by Mettoy, Rolls Razor, ROF Fazakerley and the Woolwich Royal Laboratories. The L1A2 was slightly simpler to manufacture but retained the roller follower while the magazine's body was made from two, rather than four, pieces of stamped steel and electrically welded together. The government-designed magazine is 2in longer than Sterling's magazines. Both the commercial and government-made magazines performed well, requiring little maintenance.

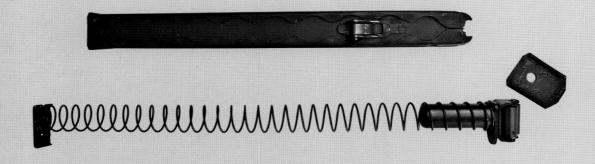

A commercial Sterling magazine disassembled for cleaning. Note the magazine's circular spring and offset roller follower. A piece of spring steel on the spine of the magazine acts as an anti-rattle device.

Suez

During Anglo-French operation to regain control of the Suez Canal zone from Egypt in 1956, Sterling submachine guns were used by both sides and met in combat for the first time. Peter Laidler notes that in 1956, Sterling released several thousand Mk 4s, originally bound for Nepal, for British use during the Suez Crisis (Laidler & Howroyd 1996: 117). A lucky few British troops were issued these new guns, but the vast majority of troops were still armed with the venerable Sten Mk V. By contrast, some troops of the Egyptian Army were armed with commercially acquired Sterling Mk 3s; this would not be the last time British troops would face adversaries also armed with Sterlings.

The Indonesian Confrontation

In 1963, Britain became embroiled in a border conflict between Malaysia and Indonesia. The Indonesian Confrontation saw Indonesia's support of Communist Kalimantan guerrillas escalate into an undeclared war, with Britain assisting Malaysian forces on the island of Borneo. The island's difficult terrain saw the war fought in dense jungle and both sides relied on small units and light-infantry tactics.

Even before the Indonesian Confrontation itself began, tensions in the region were high. In December 1962, a revolt broke out in Brunei during which insurgents from the Brunei People's Party took the British official in Limbang hostage. The British launched an operation to free the official and his family and troops were on the receiving end of fire from captured British weaponry. On 12 December, Royal Marines of L Company, 42 Commando launched a raid against rebel positions in Limbang and came under fire from L2A3 Sterlings which had been seized from the town's police station. 42 Commando made an opposed amphibious

A platoon commander and an NCO of 1st Green Jackets (43rd and 52nd) discuss defensive positions at Sapit, an Iban village, in Sarawak, Malaysia, 1964. (© IWM TR 24485-27)

A second lieutenant of The Royal Ulster Rifles discusses the next phase of the operation, Borneo, 1964. The lieutenant and the corporal to his right both have L2A3s. The lieutenant appears to have a piece of string looped around his magazine housing; this field expediency may be to loop over the bolt to prevent an accidental discharge due to the bolt being jarred when moving through thick undergrowth, or perhaps to prevent losing a loose magazine. (© IWM R 30370)

landing, taking fire from a captured Bren gun and several Sterlings. It appears that the insurgents' weapons handling was not up to British standards, however, as after-action reports described a recovered Sterling magazine with 30 rounds loaded the wrong way, inadvertently aiding the British (Chanin 2014: 155). The commandos managed to beat the insurgents back and rescue the official and his family.

The escalating confrontation with Indonesia on the Malaysian border saw a campaign of intense jungle warfare involving ambushes, patrols and brutal close-range firefights. In August 1964 one such firefight showed how the combination of bravery and the firepower of an L2A3 could mean the difference between life and death. On 29 August, the lead section of C Company, 2nd Battalion, 2nd King Edward VII's Own Gurkha Rifles (The Sirmoor Rifles) was returning to base after an unsuccessful patrol when they came under intense fire near the border just south of Kumpang Langir. As they emerged from a patch of jungle into a clearing half of the leading section was immediately killed or wounded by enemy fire, including the Bren gun team. Realizing his section had walked into an Indonesian ambush, Lance Corporal Amarjit Pun moved forward into the killing zone to grab the section's Bren gun and bring it back into action. However, as he picked it up, the Bren gun was hit by enemy rifle fire and damaged. Amarjit quickly transitioned back to his L2A3 Sterling and opened fire on the Indonesian ambush positions little more than 10yd away. He stood on the track, in the centre of the killing ground, calmly laying down suppressive fire, emptying magazine after magazine into the

48

enemy positions. Amarjit was able to achieve fire superiority long enough to allow another platoon to move up, break up the Indonesian ambush and chase the enemy back over the border. For his bravery Lance Corporal Amarjit was awarded the Military Medal. Amarjit's actions show just how formidable the Sterling's firepower could be at close range.

On 8 December 1964, a Royal Marine patrol operating from rubber boats was ambushed as it landed near the Malaysia–Indonesia border on Sebatik Island. The patrol leader, Lieutenant Robert Seeger, was wounded in the right arm by the first burst of enemy fire. Despite being wounded he charged the Indonesian position while firing bursts from his Sterling. Under heavy fire Seeger silenced an enemy machine gun and then led an attack through the Indonesian defensive position. This small action was typical of the jungle skirmishes in which British troops were engaged during the Confrontation. Seeger was awarded the Military Cross for his bravery and leadership. The conflict finally came to an end in August 1966, following protracted negotiations that saw Indonesia eventually accept the sovereignty of Malaysia.

Aden

During the Aden Emergency (1962–67), British troops were involved in another difficult counter-insurgency campaign in the port of Aden and the surrounding hinterland. The Sterling was routinely issued to patrols, military police and those detailed to accompany Intelligence Officers and

A combined-services patrol made up of personnel from the Women's Royal Army Corps, the Royal Military Police and the Royal Navy Police patrols the Crater, 1965. Military-police patrols were typically armed with pistols and Sterling submachine guns. (© IWM TR 24297)

Use of the Sterling was not confined to the Crater during the Aden Emergency; it also saw action during operations in the Radfan Mountains to the north of the city. In this photograph a radio operator from 1st Battalion, The Royal Sussex Regiment stands by armed with an L2A3 while his company commander uses the radio. (© IWM ADN 65-355-64)

members of Aden Police's Special Branch on raids. Those armed with the compact Sterling could easily and rapidly enter and exit vehicles; the weapon was readily concealable and short enough to be handy in the confined spaces of the narrow streets, bars and cafes of the claustrophobic urban area of Aden known as the Crater.

The L2A3 was extensively used by the Royal Military Police, Special Branch and Special Air Service snatch squads that operated in the Crater. The Sterling was found to be an ideal, compact weapon for these units which had to move fast to arrest suspects. Corporal Charles Russell of 1st The Queen's Dragoon Guards recalled one such operation to pick up insurgent suspects, during which he and half a dozen colleagues, all in plain clothes and armed with Sterlings, were accompanied by a Special Branch officer and an Arab constable (Walker 2011: 184). Lance Corporal Terry Cheek was also assigned to one of these parties; armed with Sterlings and Browning Hi-Power pistols, they searched for insurgent weapons caches. During a search operation one of Cheek's team spotted a suspect, a known bomber, evading the patrol; the soldier opened fire with his Sterling at 50yd and hit the fleeing suspect (Walker 2011: 184).

The British forces in Aden worked very closely with members of the Aden Police's Special Branch. So effective were some of these officers that in August 1965, Arab insurgents began an assassination campaign specifically targeting Special Branch officers. Superintendent R.L. Waggit was attacked at his home when a gunman fired a pistol through his front door into the living room where Waggit was listening to the radio. Luckily for Waggit, his alert bodyguard managed to push him out of the way and fire a burst from his Sterling through the door, driving off the gunman.

With a large number of checkpoints searching residents of Aden for weapons and explosives daily there was a need for female personnel to search Arab women. Private Pauline Cole, a switchboard operator, was one of the few female British soldiers in Aden and was frequently detailed to the checkpoints. When a British outpost came under fire Private Cole was handed an L2A3 and ordered outside, where she was urged to fire the weapon. Cole proved to be more than capable with her Sterling, hitting about five opponents before they retired into the sand dunes (Cole 2015: 32).

By 1967, the situation in Aden had deteriorated rapidly as the British prepared to pull out. On 20 June, the South Arabian Army and police in Aden mutinied, taking control of the Police Barracks and its armoury and ambushing British troops on the streets. As a convoy of Land Rovers from 1st Battalion, The Royal Northumberland Fusiliers approached the police barracks the mutinous police opened fire on them. As the vehicles took fire they halted and the Fusiliers baled out; fire from insurgents in the surrounding buildings was intense, killing and wounding several men. Twenty-year-old Fusilier John Storey took cover and began to return fire with his Sterling. Wounded several times, he dived into a nearby block of flats; climbing to the roof to see if relief was coming, he spotted two Arab insurgents on the rooftop of the next building firing on a British reconnaissance helicopter flying overhead. Storey put his Sterling on full-automatic and fired a burst at one of the insurgents, who fell backwards as the second man took cover (Walker 2011: 245). Storey kept up his fire on the insurgent positions surrounding him, but he soon ran out of ammunition and was eventually captured.

Earlier in the day, Storey had seen several armoured cars from 1st The Queen's Dragoon Guards pass by. The commander of one of these armoured cars, 2nd Lieutenant Nigel Stevens, stopped near the building in which Storey was hiding, but was unaware there was a survivor in hiding. When his vehicle reached the junction where the Fusiliers' Land Rovers had been ambushed, it came under heavy rifle and machine-gun fire from the surrounding rooftops. Stevens had not yet been authorized to use his armoured car's main armament; instead, he engaged enemy positions with his Sterling from the vehicle's top hatch. This had limited effect and the armoured vehicles were ordered to pull out of the town and British troops did not re-enter for several weeks. Finally, in November 1967, British forces withdrew from Aden and the independent People's Republic of South Yemen was formed.

Northern Ireland

The Sterling saw extensive service in Northern Ireland during the British Army's 38-year-long Operation *Banner*. The L2A3 was routinely carried by British troops, while officers of the Royal Ulster Constabulary (RUC) were also issued the Sterling Mk 4. Operation *Banner* began on 14 August 1969, when the Army was tasked with a peacekeeping role to support

Northern Irish police efforts to maintain order during escalating sectarian violence between Ulster Loyalists and Irish Republicans. At *Banner*'s peak more than 20,000 troops were deployed to Northern Ireland and generations of British soldiers served tours during The Troubles.

Sterling submachine guns may have been used in some of the early acts of sectarian violence which led to the deployment of British troops during the August 1969 Northern Ireland Riots. Joe Cahill, a member of the Provisional IRA (PIRA), alleged that members of the Ulster Special Constabulary, a reserve police force nicknamed the 'B Specials', joined a Protestant mob and indiscriminately fired upon Catholic homes near the Shankill Road area. After the initial unrest, tensions in Northern Ireland remained high and violence intermittently erupted, with the 1970s seeing much of the worst skirmishing. The following collection of incidents outlines the use of Sterlings throughout The Troubles by both insurgent and government forces.

On 15 May 1971, two British soldiers from The Royal Highland Fusiliers (Princess Margaret's Own Glasgow and Ayrshire Regiment) were wounded when they pulled over a suspicious vehicle. As the troops approached the vehicle one of the passengers, a member of the PIRA, opened fire with a stolen Sterling. The two soldiers were wounded but returned fire, killing William Reid, a PIRA officer, before the vehicle sped off.

Three months later on 18 August, during a barricade-clearing operation in the Bogside, Derry/Londonderry, men of the 17/21st Lancers came under fire from PIRA gunmen. Soldiers returned fire and one gunman, Eamonn Lafferty, was wounded by fire from an L2A3. A Royal Armoured Corps' Air Squadron helicopter operating overhead saw Lafferty being evacuated by a car. The helicopter crew were able to coordinate a roadblock which eventually apprehended three terrorists and found that the wounded gunman had died.

On 27 August 1973, Private Kenneth Hill of the Ulster Defence Regiment (UDR) was killed in a PIRA ambush. Following a report of a possible car bomb an RUC officer armed with a Sterling submachine gun and UDR personnel, including Hill, had been called to evacuate part of a housing estate in Armagh. While providing security and awaiting a bomb-disposal unit PIRA gunmen opened fire. Private Hill was killed and two UDR corporals were wounded. The RUC officer quickly took cover behind a wall. Spotting the PIRA gunmen's muzzle flashes the RUC officer returned fire with his Sterling before he too was wounded.

Over the course of nearly 40 years of violence during The Troubles the Sterling was also employed by paramilitary groups from both sides of the sectarian divide. The guns were often used in attacks on civilians. On 20 December 1972, one such attack saw two men from the Protestant paramilitary group the Ulster Freedom Fighters burst into Annie's Bar in Top of the Hill, Derry/Londonderry. The bar was full of customers watching a football match when the two gunmen entered, one armed with a pistol, the other with a Sterling submachine gun. Firing in bursts, the gunmen sprayed the bar, killing one Protestant man and four Catholic men and wounding four more before fleeing the scene.

The Sterling was well regarded for its firepower and relatively compact size and those used by the paramilitary groups on both sides were invariably stolen from the authorities – either from UDR battalion armouries, with the help of sympathizers, or from the homes of RUC officers and members of the UDR. Insurgents often targeted the homes of men they knew kept their weapons at home. In September 1972, the PIRA launched a spate of attacks on the homes of UDR members. Private Darling's wife opened the door to a group of gunmen who ransacked her house while her husband was at work. Mrs Darling had managed to hide her husband's Sterling under their bed along with their children. On 23 October 1972, the UDR barracks at Kings Park Camp in Lurgan were raided by members of the Ulster Volunteer Force (UVF). Having disarmed guards at the camp they gained entry to the unit's armoury and stole 85 L1A1 rifles and 21 L2A3 submachine guns. While a substantial amount of the UVF's haul was later recovered a large number of guns, including 15 L2A3s, remained at large. Ballistic tests later showed that 11 shootings had been carried out with just one of the Sterlings stolen from the UDR barracks.

Nearly 150 weapons were stolen in 1972 and another 55 were lost in 1973. These weapons were inevitably put to use. On the night of 31 May/1 June 1973, Loyalist gunmen launched a wave of attacks on Catholic pubs in Belfast. One of the guns used to spray customers in Muldoon's Bar, killing one man, was a UDR Sterling stolen eight months earlier.

On the evening of 3 February 1973, Loyalist gunmen launched a series of attacks on Catholic areas of Belfast. Two PIRA volunteers, James Sloan and James McCann, were killed when Loyalist gunmen opened fire on Lynch's Bar on the New Lodge Road. The two men had allegedly been shot with a stolen Sterling.

The scale of PIRA operations grew and on 30 August 1973, the East Tyrone PIRA Brigade attacked the border village of Pettigoe, placing bombs in the village's garage and post office and lining up residents, asking their names and religious affiliation. Private Mervyn Johnston, a

UDR member, managed to escape the gunmen under a hail of fire. He raced home, seized his L2A3 and engaged the PIRA members until they retreated over the Irish border. Both of the bombs later detonated, destroying the garage and post office and killing British bomb-disposal expert Staff Sergeant Ron Beckett. Johnston was subsequently awarded the Military Medal for his bravery.

In response to the escalating situation the British Government decided to deploy SAS counter-terrorism specialists, with operations officially beginning in Northern Ireland in 1976. The SAS teams frequently used the Sterling during raids and surveillance operations. On 24 November 1978, SAS troopers armed with Sterlings, with flashlights taped to their muzzles, confronted Patrick Duffy, a PIRA member, killing him as he checked an arms cache in an empty house in Derry/Londonderry.

On 16 March 1978, Francis Hughes, a particularly vicious PIRA officer, was wounded by fire from an L2A3 during a firefight near an abandoned farm building near Maghera, County Derry/Londonderry. Hughes and his men had been out on patrol and on their return inadvertently ran into an observation post manned by two members of The Parachute Regiment. The two British soldiers were both wounded, one mortally, in the short firefight that ensued; Hughes was also badly wounded in the legs and was found hiding in some bushes the next morning.

Unlike the semi-automatic L1A1 rifle, the Sterling was capable of both semi- and fully automatic fire, and when the blood was up and adrenaline pumping it was easy for troops to loose off a full magazine when they made contact with the enemy. Remembering a contact during a foot patrol in Belfast in the early 1970s, a corporal from The Royal Green Jackets recalled being in Cyprus Street in the evening and hearing a couple of low-velocity shots before the situation quickly escalated. He fired 30 or so rounds from his Sterling, changing magazines instinctively (Arthur 1987: 53).

Sometimes the Sterling's firepower was the difference between life and death for those who carried it as a personal weapon. On 28 June 1978, two RUC officers challenged a group of men placing a bomb into a stolen vehicle. As the officers moved to investigate the car, a gunman opened fire on them. The two RUC officers dived for cover; one returned fire with his Sterling, suppressing the gunmen and forcing them to jump into a waiting car and speed off. The RUC, later re-formed as the Police Service of Northern Ireland, used the Sterling Mk 4 from 1971 until 1992, when it was replaced with Heckler & Koch's MP5.

Operation *Banner*, 1972 (opposite)

Officers of the Royal Ulster Constabulary supported by British troops, man a stop-and-search checkpoint on a road in Belfast. An RUC officer armed with an L2A3 Sterling covers a suspect as his colleague discovers an unloaded homemade submachine gun hidden in the vehicle. The homemade 'Shipyard Special', built by Loyalist paramilitary groups, is a crudely made copy of the British Sterling, utilizing captured or stolen Sterling magazines – easily recognizable by their characteristic curve. An RUC officer holds up the illegal weapon as British soldiers, armed with L1A1 self-loading rifles, search other vehicles stopped by the checkpoint.

Two views of a 'Shipyard Special' submachine gun, courtesy of the Light Weapons Wing, Defence Academy of the UK. Weapons such as this one were built from readily available tube metal and cannibalized parts from stolen Sterlings, including the grips, bolt and magazine. This 'homemade' Sterling lacks a stock and is significantly lighter than the real thing.

At the height of The Troubles both the Republicans and Loyalists sought any weapons they could lay their hands on. These ranged from smuggled AR-18 assault rifles and stolen police revolvers to crude but ingenious homemade submachine guns colloquially known as 'Shipyard Specials'. These weapons, often styled after the Sterling, were made from tube steel and scavenged parts and frequently used the Sterling's curved magazines.

Operation *Banner* finally came to an end in July 2007; operations began to be scaled down following the 1998 Good Friday Agreement and while the peace process is ongoing, relative stability has returned to Northern Ireland. *Banner* has the distinction of being the longest continuous deployment in the British Army's history.

The Falklands War

The early hours of 2 April 1982 saw one of the rare instances when Sterling submachine guns clashed with each other. Some of the Royal Marines defending Government House in Port Stanley were armed with the standard-issue L2A3, while some of the attacking Argentine Agrupación de Comandos Anfibios were armed with both Dagenham-made commercial Sterling Mk 4s and suppressed Sterling-Patchett Mk 5s.

The Royal Marine garrison tasked with defending the Falkland Islands had received warning of the impending Argentine invasion and had taken up defensive positions in key locations, one of which was Government House. Once it was realized the invasion was imminent every man counted; even the ten naval hydrographers left behind by HMS *Endurance*, before she headed for South Georgia, were issued Sterlings and quickly taught how to use them. The hydrographers helped man the defences at Government House when the Argentine commandos arrived.

While some Argentine commandos attacked the empty Royal Marine barracks at Moody Brook another platoon under Lieutenant-Commander Pedro Giachino advanced on Government House from positions on the rocky hillock that overlooked it. Intending to infiltrate the house and snatch the Governor, Giachino led a five-man team to the rear of the building. The Royal Marines of Naval Party 8901 dug in at Government House quickly spotted the enemy snatch team and opened fire. Giachino and another commando were quickly wounded, the snatch team retreated and a medic who attempted to reach the mortally wounded Giachino was also injured by a grenade.

During a lull in the fighting for Government House, Major Gary Noott was checking the Royal Marines' defensive positions when he heard Spanish voices above him. Three members of the Agrupación de Comandos Anfibios had managed to infiltrate Government House during the first skirmish and had remained hidden during the early hours of the morning. Major Noott decided to oust the Argentine commandos. Setting his Sterling to what he thought was automatic he fired through the ceiling, but when he pulled the trigger there was only a single bang. Noott had not pushed the selector lever all the way forward to the fully automatic position. Another Royal Marine, realizing Noott's mistake, quickly fired a burst from his own Sterling, causing the hidden Argentine commandos to hurry downstairs and surrender (Bound 2007: 66). Several hours later, with the main Argentine landing force approaching, Governor Sir Rex

Defending Government House, 2 April 1982 (overleaf)

Royal Marines of Naval Party 8901 defend Government House in Port Stanley against a dawn attack by Argentine commandos. Two Royal Marines open fire on a group of approaching Argentine commandos led by Lieutenant-Commander Pedro Giachino. The clash saw Sterlings used on both sides. One of the Royal Marines opens fire with his L2A3 while the other aims his L1A1 self-loading rifle. The Argentine commandos are armed with a mix of weapons including a commercial suppressed Sterling-Patchett Mk 5, an Uzi and a commercial Sterling Mk 4. The Argentine attack was beaten off, but the commandos laid siege to Government House until their main force arrived at 0930hrs compelling the governor of the Falkland Islands, Sir Rex Hunt, to surrender.

Hunt ordered Naval Party 8901 to lay down their arms and surrender. By 0800hrs Port Stanley had been occupied. The British Government decided to retake the islands and a Task Force was despatched from Britain.

The British Task Force to retake the islands arrived on 21 May 1982, and the Sterling quickly saw action again. As companies of 2nd Battalion, The Parachute Regiment (2 PARA), part of 3 Commando Brigade who were the first to land, prepared to climb into landing craft, they checked their kit and some loaded their weapons. Allegedly, a Sterling was negligently discharged as the men waited; luckily, the round only grazed a soldier's foot, but no doubt did little to settle the men's nerves.

The windswept, featureless marshland of the Falklands was not the ideal ground for the Sterling. Effective out to a maximum of 200m (219yd), the gun did not have the reach of the 7.62×51mm L1A1 self-loading rifles or GPMGs. Like many soldiers, Jim Love of 2 PARA knew that the Sterling was best used at close range. Faced with the open expanses of the Falklands, Love recalled that several of his colleagues had left their Sterlings behind owing to the weapon's limited range.

During Goose Green, the first land battle of the war, 2 PARA was ordered to attack over open ground towards Darwin Hill. During the battle, the battalion's commander, Lieutenant-Colonel Herbert 'H' Jones, led from the front armed with an L2A3 Sterling. Seeing his leading company pinned down by Argentine rifle and machine-gun fire, Jones and his covering party pushed up the Darwin Hill ridgeline to clear some enemy trenches in a flanking attack. Jones, known for leading from the front, charged up the slope firing his submachine gun from the hip. Sergeant Major Barry Norman recalled seeing Jones charging towards the enemy trench, armed with his Sterling. As Jones moved forwards he was exposed to fire from other Argentine positions; only 6ft or so from the trench, Jones was shot from the enemy trenches behind him (Bishop 2002: 52). Major Tony Rice of the Royal Artillery accompanied Jones and his cover party during the battle, and also witnessed Jones' ill-fated attack on the Argentine positions. Rice saw Jones roll down the hill, rise to his feet and fit a full magazine to his Sterling before resuming his attack on the enemy trench; Jones was hit again just before reaching the trench (Fitz-Gibbon 2001: 116). The trench from which Jones had been shot was later destroyed by a 66mm light anti-tank rocket. Lieutenant-Colonel Jones was awarded a posthumous Victoria Cross for his gallantry.

As 2 PARA pushed towards the Argentine airfield and the occupied village of Goose Green, enemy soldiers began to surrender. Lieutenant James Barry, a platoon commander from D Company, was attempting to take two Argentine soldiers prisoner when he was caught in crossfire and killed. The Argentine troops he had been calling on to surrender thought they were being fired upon and immediately opened fire, killing Barry. Lieutenant Barry's radio operator, Private Knight, reacted instantly, opening fire at close range with his L2A3 and killing the two Argentines. While the Sterling may not have been well suited to the long-range firefights in which British troops in the Falklands sometimes found themselves, the submachine guns were in their element during these close-range trench-clearing engagements.

The infantry fighting in the Falklands were not the only ones equipped with the Sterling; other rear-echelon units issued the L2A3 as a personal defence weapon included the Royal Artillery, Royal Army Ordnance Corps, Royal Engineers, Army Air Corps and even members of the Royal Army Medical Corps. Having witnessed the fighting at Goose Green Captain Steven Hughes, 2 PARA's Regimental Medical Officer, armed himself with a pistol and an L2A3 submachine gun for the rest of the campaign.

The Sterling once again came into its own during the bitter fighting to clear the Argentine positions on Mount Longdon. During the night assault, Company Sergeant-Major John Weeks entered an enemy bunker and was immediately suspicious when he spotted a body on the ground with a blanket covering it. Weeks handed his Sterling to a corporal and ordered him to open fire if there was any sign of movement when he lifted the blanket; the man under the blanket moved to release a phosphorus

British troops practise their weapons handling aboard the cruise liner *Queen Elizabeth II* while en route to retake the Falklands. The two men in the foreground have L2A3s; the second man is in the process of loading a magazine. (JDHC Archive/Getty Images)

grenade but was immediately shot by the corporal covering Weeks. The fighting for the summit of Mount Longdon was a brutal battle conducted at close quarters. Weeks recalled how, after jumping into an Argentine trench he thought cleared, he was startled when he saw an enemy soldier move. Reacting instantaneously, Weeks nearly hit his own foot as he opened fire on the Argentine whose trench he'd just jumped into. This was the kind of fighting the submachine gun had been developed for at the end of World War I. The Sterling's firepower and compact size proved ideal for clearing Argentine bunkers and trenches (Arthur 1985: 302).

Elsewhere during the battle Private Dean Coady, along with two other soldiers, had cleared two Argentine trenches when he was wounded in the right arm by shrapnel from one of his own grenades. Continuing on, Coady realized his arm was feeling numb. Increasingly unable to hold his rifle properly, he asked another member of his section who was armed with an L2A3 if he could swap his L1A1 for the lighter submachine gun. After swapping, Coady pressed on and cleared another enemy position.

It was not just on land that the Sterling saw action during operations in the Falklands. On 21 May, the Type 21 frigate HMS *Ardent* was on station in San Carlos Water when she came under air attack from Argentine A-4 Skyhawks. Armed with 1,000lb bombs, the Skyhawks attacked *Ardent* and another frigate, HMS *Yarmouth*. *Ardent*'s Sea Cat anti-aircraft missile system failed to lock on to the attacking aircraft and they were able to score several hits on the frigate, destroying the Sea Cat launcher. *Ardent*'s 4.5in gun proved ineffective against the attacking aircraft and in a desperate effort to defend the ship Lieutenant Commander John Murray Sephton, commander of *Ardent*'s helicopter crew, organized the use of small arms, directing fire against the Skyhawks.

A final wave of Argentine Navy Skyhawks attacked scoring two direct hits on the stern of *Ardent*, and it was this wave that Lieutenant Commander Sephton and his men engaged with small arms in an attempt to defend the ship. Reportedly, Sephton stood on *Ardent*'s flight deck firing a Sterling L2A3 at a Skyhawk as it flew overhead. The bomb that this aircraft dropped struck the flight deck, killing Sephton and three other members of the crew. For his actions Sephton was posthumously awarded the Distinguished Service Cross. *Ardent* was heavily damaged and the surviving crew were evacuated before she sank the next day.

During the battle of Mount Tumbledown, as the British made the last push to recapture Port Stanley, the Sterling again came into its own. During the night attack mounted by 2nd Battalion, Scots Guards on Argentine defensive positions, the British encountered stiff resistance, being beaten back by mortar fire before they were finally able to push methodically through Argentine trenches and foxholes. Using hand grenades to clear trenches, the British cleared one of the last Argentine positions with a phosphorus grenade and bursts of fire from a section leader's L2A3. The next day, 14 June, Argentine forces on the Falklands officially surrendered.

Despite some complaints about the L2A3's lack of range and reports of ill-fitting magazines falling out of weapons, the Sterling performed well during the Falklands campaign, proving that it provided essential controllable firepower at close ranges. Even so, as British troops were fighting in the Falklands the British Army was already developing its next service rifle. A series of experimental rifles, including the XL70, XL80 and XL85, later known as the Small Arms of the 1980s or SA80, had been in development for some time. The rifle which evolved from this programme would eventually be adopted as the L85. The 5.56×45mm bullpup would soon replace both the L1A1 self-loading rifle and the L2A3 submachine gun, but not before these weapons fought one last battle.

The Gulf War

The Gulf War of 1991 saw the last hurrah for a number of British Cold War small arms including the 7.62×51mm L4 Bren light machine gun, the L1A1 self-loading rifle and the Sterling L2A3 submachine gun. The L2A3 continued to be issued to vehicle crews, support troops and anyone not issued with the old L1A1 or the new L85A1 rifle. Iraq had been one of the first major purchasers of the new Sterling Mk 4, ordering more than 13,000 weapons; this order was fulfilled between 1956 and 1964. It has been alleged that one or more of these early Sterlings may have been used to assassinate Iraq's King Faisal II during the 14 July Revolution in 1958, which saw the country become a republic. During Operation *Granby*, British troops fought through Iraqi defensive positions with a weapon, the L85A1, which did not function well in sandy conditions. Unsurprisingly, both the L2A3 and L1A1 performed far better in these conditions than the new rifle.

Twelve years later during the 2003 Iraq War, the Sterling was still in use by Saddam Hussein's regime. In July 2003, Adnan Abdullah Abid al-Muslit, one of Saddam's most trusted bodyguards, was cornered and captured by Coalition forces. During his arrest he was reported to have tried to grab a Sterling Mk 4. Coalition Special Forces also put some captured Iraqi Sterlings to good use as dash guns – attaching them to vehicles by a length of bungee cord for quick use by vehicle drivers.

While vintage small arms from World War II have been frequently documented during the recent conflicts in Syria and Iraq, sightings of the Sterling have proven rare, although some captured Mk 4s have been photographed. These are probably part of the substantial Iraqi contract from the late 1950s.

FOREIGN USERS

Throughout its history the Sterling Armament Company did its best to sell its weapons worldwide, with agents making demonstration trips to dozens of countries. As a commercial company Sterling had long relied on foreign exports, with 90 per cent of production sold overseas. Sterling frequently sent agents to demonstrate the company's wares to foreign militaries and police forces. One such agent was Major Beavan Keen, a

While this book has predominantly examined British use of the Sterling it should also be noted that commercially made Sterling submachine guns equipped military and law-enforcement personnel all around the world, from Rhodesia and Angola to Malaya and Yemen. Here, Sterling representatives supervise a demonstration to Royal Malaysian Police officers at Malaysia's National Police Training Centre during the early 1980s. A variety of Sterling Mk 4s, Mk 5s, AR-18s and revolvers are being tested. (Courtesy of the Royal Armouries)

retired Royal Marine. As sales director, Keen travelled extensively and was responsible for winning a number of large contracts. He developed a series of tricks for showing off the Sterling during demonstrations. When James Edmiston bought Sterling in 1972, he quickly moved to increase Sterling's exports. Before embarking on a sales tour in the Far East, Keen taught Edmiston some of his techniques, such as highlighting the Sterling's low recoil by resting the butt on his chin while shooting, and firing the Sterling on full-automatic while holding it in the flat palm of his hand (while gripping the bayonet boss between two fingers) to demonstrate that the weapon did not climb and lose accuracy (Edmiston 2011: 19).

Early orders for small numbers of Mk 3s for testing purposes were placed by a large number of countries including Bahrain, Brazil, Cuba, Egypt, France, Singapore, South Africa, Sweden and West Germany. Many of these countries went on to purchase larger quantities. Some of the largest purchases were made by African and Middle Eastern countries including Ghana, Iraq, Kuwait, Libya, Nigeria and Tunisia. Sales to Europe were limited, with contracts including Northern Ireland and Portugal.

In November 1955, West Germany reformed its armed forces, creating the Bundeswehr. The Bundeswehr quickly began the process of rearmament and between 1956 and 1959 ran a series of trials to adopt a new submachine gun. Sterling entered the Mk 4 into these trials, in which it competed against a number of designs including the Mauser MP-57, the Erma MP-60 and the Uzi. James Edmiston, the managing director of Sterling between 1971 and 1983, claims that the Mk 4 won the West German trials outright but the Uzi was adopted, as the MP2, for financial reasons (Edmiston 2011: 22).

THE STERLING IN VIETNAM

During the Vietnam War, Australia and New Zealand both deployed troops to South Vietnam. Some L2A3s were used by New Zealand troops, while Australian troops carried the venerable Owen Gun and the new F1 submachine gun. Suppressed Sterlings also saw use during the conflict, with CIA operatives and members of the US and Australian Special Forces favouring the Sterling-Patchett L34A1/Mk 5 for its reliability and quietness.

The Australian Special Air Service Regiment (SASR) began operations in Vietnam in 1966, and in late 1967 requested nine new L34A1 Sterling-Patchetts from Britain. The SASR squadron operating in Vietnam reported that numerous 'recce-ambush' patrols had been compromised due to premature contact with the enemy, and it was felt that a weapon capable of silencing enemy scouts quietly would improve the ambush success rate significantly. In total Australia purchased 88 Mk 5s, while New Zealand purchased a further five.

US units from Military Assistance Command Vietnam, Special Operations Group also favoured suppressed Stens and Sterlings for clandestine operations such as long-range reconnaissance patrols, prisoner snatches and assassinations. The Sten Mk II(S) was well liked because it could be disassembled easily and compactly stored in a rucksack whereas the Sterling-Patchett Mk 5 had the added advantage of a folding stock. This handy, compact package allowed operators to carry a primary weapon in addition to the Sterling.

There is some photographic evidence to suggest that members of the Australian SAS made an interesting battlefield modification to some of their L34A1 suppressed Sterlings in the form of Colt CGL-4 (XM148) 40mm grenade launchers attached to some of the guns. While this may have been barrack-room humour, contrasting the loud with the quiet, the set-up certainly maximized firepower.

The L34A1 was used by a number of special-forces units in Vietnam, favoured for its ability to kill enemy sentries or point men quietly. It was also compact enough to allow troops to carry an additional primary weapon if necessary. This example is in the collections of the Light Weapons Wing, Defence Academy of the UK.

Outside of the contract with India, which saw 32,536 Mk 4s delivered, the largest purchaser of guns from Sterling was Malaysia which bought at least 18,500 Sterling Mk 4s, these being used extensively by the country's security forces during the Second Communist Insurgency (1968–89) and by Malaysian peacekeepers deployed with the United Nations. It is a testament to the manufacturing quality and robust design of the Sterling that many of the submachine guns are still in use today over 30 years after production ended.

IMPACT
Insight and influence

THE TROOPS' VERDICT

In service with dozens of countries around the world since the early 1950s, the Sterling's robust, reliable design has withstood the test of time. While the Sterling is no longer in service with the British and Canadian militaries, Indian Ordnance Factories continue to produce Mk 4-pattern submachine guns. Perhaps the best equipped to judge the impact of a weapon are those who used it; and the men who had experience with both the Sten and the Sterling had clear opinions. Many accounts from these men make it clear that the Sterling was held in higher regard than the weapon it replaced.

John Wroath, an officer with the Royal Artillery's 29th Field Regiment during the 1950s, felt the Sterling 'was well made, it was precision engineered, whereas the Sten was literally rattle-fit engineering … the Sten gun was quite capable of going off on its own it seemed. Whereas the Sterling was much better made, altogether safer. The butt folded in, which made it much easier to carry … an altogether better weapon than the Sten' (IWM 26548). Eddie Clark of The Cameronians (Scottish Rifles), a veteran of Korea and Malaya, also felt the Sterling was 'a much more accurate weapon [than the Sten], easier to handle, I liked the Sterling' (IWM 26579). Paul Garman, then a sergeant with The Royal Norfolk Regiment, felt 'the Sterling was a much safer weapon [than the Sten], you could actually drop it on its butt and it wouldn't cock and fire … it was a much more robust weapon and proved its worth, a very useful weapon indeed.' He recalled 'it handled very much the same as the Sten gun, the drills were the same, and had a similar kind of firepower but it was a safer and more robust weapon' (IWM 24732). Similarly, Sergeant Major Jim O'Neil of 1st Battalion, The Royal Inniskilling Fusiliers who used the Sten in Malaya felt the Sterling 'was

a very good weapon for close quarter fighting, it was very accurate up to 200 yards' (IWM 32388).

In terms of accuracy, while some felt the Sterling paled in comparison with the L1A1 self-loading rifle, others recognized its capability within its limits as a submachine gun. John Lincoln, who served as an NCO in the Royal Army Dental Corps, noted 'It was quite easy, given a bit of practice, to hit consistently a Fig.11 [target] at 100m [109yd], on single shot, from kneeling supported … as long as you hold it firmly and use the time-honoured method of firing in short bursts it's reasonably accurate' (IWM 27244).

Myths surrounding the stopping power of the Sterling abound, with the tale of a wet blanket stopping 9×19mm rounds often told. Although some troops may have felt the Sterling's 9×19mm ammunition was underpowered, many – such as Martin Hornby, a Royal Marine – understood that it was 'the right weapon for the right situation'. Hornby remembered his training as a young Marine: 'when you pull the trigger it kicks right, always kicks right … controlled bursts at ideally no more than 60 metres [66yd]. It's a close quarters battle weapon … For street clearing, house clearing that sort of stuff, because an SLR is too big for that, it's too long, you're going to catch it on door frames and all sorts ...' (IWM 27047). Guy Smith, a gunner with the Royal Horse Artillery, agreed: 'because it was short and stocky … you could spray a room no problem' (IWM 27241).

Another aspect of the Sterling that many soldiers appreciated was just how much easier to clean it was when compared to the L1A1 self-loading rifle or the GPMG. Gunner Guy Smith recalled that the Sterling was 'easier to clean … [with] just a boot brush and a pull through and there you go' (IWM 27241). Like all compact submachine guns the Sterling's handiness could also prove dangerous in negligent hands, however, and many British soldiers recall sessions at the firing range when safety with the Sterling was drummed into them. Smith is one of those who recall being warned about accidentally pointing the L2A3 at other troops: 'the

ABOVE LEFT
An L2A3 stowed unloaded in an FV721 Fox armoured vehicle, just below a storage box for No. 36 hand grenades. Because of its short length the Sterling was issued as standard to vehicle crews. Bob Nelson, an NCO with 13th/18th Hussars (Queen Mary's Own), recalled being issued a Sterling: 'Being Armoured Corps, we were issued with the submachine gun, or SMG as it was known, because it was a shorter weapon and it was easier to store inside armoured fighting vehicles or tanks' (IWM 29538). L2A3s issued to Royal Armoured Corps crews were typically stowed in purpose-built racks without a magazine loaded. (The Tank Museum 8729-B3)

ABOVE RIGHT
Men of C Squadron, 1st Battalion, The Royal Tank Regiment train with their personal weapons at the Dhekelia Ranges on Cyprus, 1983. The L2A3 was the standard-issue weapon for armoured-vehicle crews. (The Tank Museum 10431-010)

A British Army officer armed with a Sterling L2A3 talks to the driver of a Land Rover during a patrol along the border between East and West Germany. The compact Sterling was the ideal length for troops clambering in and out of vehicles. (© IWM CT 1216)

problems was … it was short and stocky and if you moved an inch you'd spray the whole room' (IWM 27241).

No weapon is perfect and troops had some criticisms of the Sterling. One of the common complaints was its ability to catch on kit and camouflage nets. Some complained that despite being extremely robust the Sterling's folding stock was difficult to deploy and fold quickly. Another criticism concerned its somewhat awkward triangular profile when loaded. Bob Nelson noted that 'because of its configuration … it was very hard to stow into vehicles because it was a triangular shape rather than a flat shape' (IWM 29538). For some, its shape made the Sterling uncomfortable to carry; even so, it was significantly lighter than a L1A1 rifle or a GPMG and for those who carried it daily it simply became something that was there.

The Sterling and its contemporaries						
Type	Calibre	Magazine capacity	Rate of fire	Action	Weight	Length (stock collapsed/stock extended)
PPS-43 (Soviet Union, 1942)	7.62×25mm	35	700rd/min	Blowback	6.8lb	24.4in/32.2in
Owen Gun (Australia, 1942)	9×19mm	32	700rd/min	Blowback	9.7lb	31.9in
Sten Mk V (UK, 1944)	9×19mm	32	550rd/min	Blowback	8.5lb	29.9in
Carl Gustav m/45 (Sweden, 1945)	9×19mm	36	600rd/min	Blowback	7.5lb	21.6in/31.9in
BSA Machine Carbine (UK, 1949)	9×19mm	32	600rd/min	Blowback	6.5lb	18.9in/27.5in
MAT-49 (France, 1949)	9×19mm	20 or 32	600rd/min	Blowback	7.7lb	18.1in/28.4in
Madsen M50 (Denmark, 1950)	9×19mm	32	550rd/min	Blowback	6.9lb	20.8in/31.5in
Uzi (Israel, 1954)	9×19mm	20, 25 or 32	600rd/min	Blowback	8.2lb	18.5in/25.6in
Sterling L2A3 (UK, 1955)	9×19mm	34	550rd/min	Blowback	6lb	19.3in/26.8in
Beretta PM12 (Italy, 1959)	9×19mm	20 or 30	550rd/min	Blowback	7lb	16.5in/25.9in
Walther MPL (Germany, 1963)	9×19mm	32	550rd/min	Blowback	6.6lb	19.3in/29.5in
Heckler & Koch MP5 (Germany, 1966)	9×19mm	15 or 30	800rd/min	Roller-delayed blowback	6.3lb	19.3in/25.9in
Ingram M10 (USA, 1970)	.45 ACP or 9×19mm	30	1,145rd/min	Blowback	6.2lb	11in/21.6in

COPIES AND CLONES

The impact of the Sterling can be measured not only in its commercial sales but also in the number of licensed – and unlicensed – copies made around the world. Not only has George Patchett's design been cloned outright, it has also influenced the design of a plethora of other weapons developed during the Cold War.

The Canadian Sterling: the C1

By the mid-1950s military planners in Canada, as in Britain, began to recognize the need for a new submachine gun to replace its ageing Sten Mk IIs. In the late 1940s, Canadian designers developed an indigenous submachine gun, the XP54. The British evaluated the XP54 in 1946 and 1948 and were intrigued by its unusual horizontal magazine. Brigadier John Arthur Barlow, the Director of Artillery (Small Arms), felt the XP54 had promise, noting that it had functioned well during preliminary testing. Despite this initial interest the XP54 suffered a number of failures and stoppages during testing, with a bulged barrel and stoppages caused by friction on misaligned parts in the weapon's horizontal magazine. As a result, further trials were cancelled.

The Canadian Army tested the Patchett in Korea and recommended it for limited adoption by units in the field. As such in November 1956, the first Anglo-Canadian Submachine Gun Steering Committee meeting was held. The Canadians requested a manufacturing licence, but wished to make some changes to the weapon before they adopted it. On 20 December, the *Ottawa Citizen* newspaper announced the Canadian Army's intention to adopt the Sterling, reporting that during extensive all-weather testing it had been found to perform better than all its peers.

The desired changes included a smaller bayonet boss and redesigned lug reinforcement for the L1A1 rifle bayonet, a simpler trigger mechanism designed by Sterling engineer Les Ruffell, a height-adjustable front sight taken from the L1A1 and protected by square sight protectors, and an adjustable rear sight with wider sight protectors. In early 1957, these changes were encapsulated in a sample model assembled from ROF Fazakerley-made L2A3s; this pattern was re-designated the L2A4 by the British.

The primary internal departures from George Patchett's original design were the decision to have a single rather than double return spring and to use a non-helically grooved bolt. Instead, the C1 used an improved Sten breech block. These changes had a number of advantages including being able to use existing tooling, avoiding paying royalties for Patchett's patented bolt and simplifying production. Compared to the Sterling-made guns the C1 was certainly simpler, using stampings and spot-welding. The C1 retained a surprising level of commonality, however, with many parts interchangeable between Canadian and British weapons. This commonality included magazines, although the Canadians also simplified the magazine's design. They dispensed with Patchett's roller system and designed their own magazine which held 30, rather than 34 rounds, but could be used in all Sterling-pattern guns.

An interesting testament to the C1's reliability came in the summer of 1990. The Army Reserve Training Camp at Camp Vernon, British Columbia, was directed to destroy its remaining stores of 9×19mm blank ammunition as it was surplus to requirements once the C1 was retired. It was decided that during infantry manoeuvre exercises the 'opposition force' (armed with C1s) would use up the remaining stocks of blank ammunition. With an abundance of surplus ammunition, the eight-man section simulating the enemy force during the four-month training tour were able to be very liberal with their ammunition; and wanting to see just how much punishment the C1 could take, they frequently forwent the usual end-of-day cleaning of their weapons. Corporal Rob Deans, one of the soldiers acting as 'the enemy' during the training exercises, recalled firing roughly 2,000 rounds of ammunition during the day – so many rounds that his C1 began to suffer stoppages. On inspecting the weapon Deans found that carbon from the blanks had accumulated under the extractor, meaning it would not seat fully and failed to grip the rim of the round; but after stripping and cleaning the weapon thoroughly it was returned to full working order. Blanks are notoriously dirty and it is a testament to the C1's, and by extension the Sterling's, design that the weapon continued functioning after firing so many rounds, in what Deans described as four months of the hardest-possible usage.

The Chilean Sterling

Throughout the 1960s and 1970s Chile was racked by political turmoil, but Sterling's records show the purchase of one Sterling Mk 4 and no fewer than 101 Mk 5s in the early 1970s. In September 1973, a military junta, led by General Augusto Pinochet, took control of the

The prototype PAF, in the collections of the Light Weapons Wing, Defence Academy of the UK. The PAF lacked the Mk 4's perforated barrel jacket and instead had an exposed barrel, tipped with a rudimentary spoon-shaped compensator. It also lacked the Sterling's folding stock, instead having a simple collapsing stock. As a result, the disassembly catch was moved to the left side of the receiver. Like the original, the Chilean copy retained the dirt-clearing grooves cut into the breech block. The PAF's plastic charging handle and buttstock were reminiscent of the Heckler & Koch MP5. The profile of the PAF's pistol grip was slightly different but the weapon still fed from standard 34-round Sterling magazines.

country via a bloody coup and all exports of small arms from Britain to Chile ceased.

In the mid-1970s the state-owned firearms manufacturer Fábricas y Maestranzas del Ejército (FAMAE) experimented with copying the Sterling Mk 4. The resulting submachine gun was dubbed the PAF or 'Pistola Ametralladora FAMAE'. It took the Sterling's basic design and simplified it. The PAF weighed 5.5lb, significantly less than the British original, and reportedly had a much higher rate of fire – 800rd/min. Only a limited number of toolroom-made prototypes appear to have been assembled and the PAF did not go into general production.

The Indian Sterling

In the late 1950s the Indian Army tested a pair of Sterling Mk 4s and in 1961, approached Sterling and the British Government to purchase a manufacturing licence. The result was an agreement that saw the Indian Government purchase technical drawings, tooling and gauges for £16,000 – a contract worth around £340,000 today. In addition to the design and tooling, the Indian Small Arms Factory at Kanpur would be able to manufacture Mk 4s without paying royalties; in return, India would purchase its first 60,000 guns from Sterling to be transferred through the British Ministry of Supply as 'aid'. With tensions on India's northern borders with Pakistan and China rising, the need to improve India's infantry weapons was becoming critical.

Of the 60,000 Mk 4s, Sterling had manufactured 51,000 before the British Government revoked the export licence when India went to war with Pakistan in 1965. Some 18,466 guns awaiting transfer to India immediately became property of the British Crown. This proved to be a thorn in Sterling's side for almost a decade as the British Government sold off the Indian Sterlings at cost price. This effectively placed the British Government in direct competition with Sterling. Some of the guns were also stripped for spare parts for the British military, an action which deprived Sterling of a substantial spare-parts contract. It was not until 1973 that Sterling was able to buy back the remaining Mk 4 guns.

India's Small Arms Factory (SAF) has since produced over a million Mk 4s, designated in Indian service the 1A Carbine. While they are built to the original drawings purchased from Sterling the fit and finish is not of the same standard, with few of the parts interchangeable with British or Canadian Sterlings. Despite this the guns have served the Indian military well for over 50 years, seeing action in conflicts with Pakistan and China as well as an insurgency in Kashmir and peacekeeping operations in Sri Lanka. Unlike Britain, India has continued to use the term 'machine carbine' rather than 'submachine gun'. Commonly known as the SAF Carbine, the 1A is largely issued to officers, NCOs, radio operators and support troops. In the 1980s approximately 130 1As were issued per infantry battalion.

Production continues at the state-owned ordnance factory in Kanpur, which since the early 2000s has produced the improved 1A1, which adds a safety sear to prevent bolt bounce. The overall manufacturing quality of the weapons has declined, however, with the fit and finish becoming cruder and the original crackle paint finish replaced by a black enamel. Kanpur also produces a copy of the suppressed L34, the 2A1, which has a canvas cover rather than a wooden foregrip.

India remains the last country actively to produce and use George Patchett's submachine gun; with over 1 million 1A Carbines produced it will continue in service for some time yet. While officially the 1A is being phased out of Indian Army service many are still in use. The Army, Navy and police and border forces all continue to use the SAF despite the introduction of newer weapons. The 1A looks set to be replaced in Indian service by the Modern Sub Machine Carbine (MSMC), developed by India's Armament Research and Development Establishment for production at the ordnance factory at Tiruchirappalli. The MSMC is gas operated and chambers a proprietary 5.56×30mm round.

Spanish Sterlings

The Sterling's influence also reached Spain where two weapons from major manufacturers shared characteristics with George Patchett's design.

The Star Z-63, the 9×19mm commercial export version of the ZB-62 which was adopted by the Spanish military. (Courtesy of Rock Island Auction Company)

Both weapons have been used by the Spanish police, armed forces and Guarda Civil.

The first of the two designs, the Star Z-62, first developed in 1962, was produced by Star Bonifacio Echeverria and introduced in the mid-1960s. The Z-62 took some of the Sterling's physical characteristics and combined them with some proprietary features. These included an interesting two-finger trigger, a recessed firing pin in the bolt which only protruded once the bolt was fully in battery and a non-reciprocating, folding charging handle which ran through the left side of the perforated barrel jacket. The Z-62 uses a single recoil spring rather than the two used by the Sterling. The Z-62's bolt also differed in that it is not cut with Patchett's helical grooves and it has a plunger in the bolt face which depresses a flap; this is designed to prevent accidental slam fires.

The Z-62's trigger mechanism, derived from the earlier Z-45, included a cross-bolt safety and a two-finger trigger which acted as fire selector. Pulling with the top finger enabled fully automatic fire; pulling the lower part of the trigger allowed semi-automatic fire. Unlike the Sterling, the Z-62 had a conventional vertical magazine housing and fed from a 30-round proprietary double-stack, double-feed magazine. The folding stock was also simpler but less robust, although it retained the Sterling's tube receiver and perforated barrel jacket. The sights and end-cap design remained largely the same as those of the British submachine guns, but the Z-62 had a conical muzzle piece which held the barrel in place. A commercial version of the Z-62 chambered in 9×19mm, the Z-63, was also exported. The Z-62 was succeeded by the Z-70/B which replaced the earlier trigger mechanism with a conventional trigger and a combined fire selector and safety lever.

Developed in the early 1960s and produced by the Centro de Estudios Técnicos de Materiales Especiales (CETME) state arsenal, the simpler C2 had a number of differences and similarities to the Sterling. While the C2's bolt was helically grooved like the Sterling's it also had a special safety feature: the firing pin was activated by a lever inside the bolt and could only protrude once the bolt was properly in battery. The C2 also had a different trigger mechanism and a distinctly profiled pistol grip with finger grooves. It used a straight 30-round magazine, but retained the Sterling's horizontal, angled magazine housing to aid feeding; and it used Sterling's tube receiver with its perforated barrel jacket and end-cap design. CETME's design also had a slightly different folding stock which locked in place using the Sterling's locking method, as well as a folding cocking handle and a sliding dust cover. Unlike the Sterling the C2's sights were set at 50m (55yd) and 100m (109yd). Like the Star, it used the commercial Sterling's crackle paint finish. It was chambered in either 9×19mm for export or 9×23mm Largo for domestic use. The C2, or CB-64 in Spanish service, replaced the Star Z-series of submachine guns in service during the 1980s. Some of the Star and CETME submachine guns remain in limited second-line Spanish service today, although they have largely been superseded by the Star Z-84 and the MP5.

The Sterling's Australian cousin: The F1

Australian representatives had been observers during the Anglo-Canadian Submachine Gun Steering Committee meetings which led to the C1. Some men of The Royal Australian Regiment had also had the chance to examine and use Patchett Mk IIs in Korea in 1953, during field trials. Australia did not adopt the Sterling, however. Instead, in 1959, a new series of designs designated the 'X' series were developed. The first two designs developed into the X3, which in 1962 was adopted as the F1.

Australian Ordnance had begun searching for a replacement for the ageing Owen Gun after the Korean War. The Owen had been made quickly and cheaply during World War II and while it was supremely reliable and had been well liked by Australian troops it was felt that a new, improved weapon was needed. Maintenance of the older Owen Guns proved difficult as each weapon had been hand-fitted to speed up production, with the result that many parts proved not to be interchangeable.

While much of the F1's design differed significantly from the original Sterling it borrowed a number of features, including the tube receiver and perforated barrel jacket, and its magazine housing profile was copied directly from the Sterling in order to ensure magazine commonality with both Britain and Canada. The only difference was that the F1's magazine housing was located on the top of the receiver in accordance with the Australian preference established by the Owen Gun.

The F1 entered service alongside the Australian L1A1 rifle, sharing a common pistol grip and control layout with the rifle as well as the same butt plate – fostering familiarity and minimizing additional unique parts needed by the submachine gun.

Like the Sterling, the F1 was a select-fire, blowback submachine gun. Its key mechanical difference was that it had a non-reciprocating bolt handle. The cocking handle was positioned on the left side of the receiver with its slot protected from the ingress of dirt by a dust cover. Although the F1 could feed from straight Sten and Owen magazines, it was issued with a 34-round curved magazine. The Australian Government had

This F1 is in the collections of the Light Weapons Wing, Defence Academy of the UK. It was heavier than its British cousin, weighing just over 7lb, and also slightly longer at 28in. Unlike the Sterling it had a fixed, solid buttstock. The F1 was first issued to Australian troops in April 1963, and despite having a top-mounted magazine – a position that lent itself to prone firing and made carrying the gun more comfortable when slung – it was not as well-liked as the Owen Gun. Many disliked the lack of a front handgrip, while others found it harder to point and aim than the Owen Gun (Wardman 1991: 156–58). The F1 had an in-line stock and as such needed raised sights. The rear sight folded against the receiver when not in use while the front sight, rather than being over the muzzle, projected from the right side of the magazine housing. The F1 could also mount the L1A1 self-loading rifle's standard L1A2 bayonet.

THE STERLING ON SCREEN

Making its screen debut in *The IPCRESS File* (1965), the Sterling appeared in numerous James Bond films starting with *You Only Live Twice* (1967), and also featured in cult classics such as *When Eight Bells Toll* (1971), *The Wild Geese* (1978) and *RoboCop* (1987). Its most iconic role, however, came when armourers of Bapty & Co. converted a number of Mk 4s to become the BlasTech E-11 blaster rifles used by Imperial stormtroopers in the first three Star Wars films: *A New Hope* (1977), *The Empire Strikes Back* (1980) and *Return of the Jedi* (1983). Both firing and non-firing prop blasters were made for the films, the external additions varying from weapon to weapon. Approximately 20 Sterling Mk 4s were retrofitted for *A New Hope*. While the blasters were assembled from available parts, the majority had an American M38 azimuth tank 'scope fixed to the top of the receiver with a special custom-made mount. A Hengstler industrial counter box was attached to the left side of the receiver and two small cylinders were added on top of the magazine housing. A series of ribs were fixed to the perforated barrel jacket and the distinct look of the blaster was completed using the much shorter ten-round magazine which was used in the live-firing guns.

The Sterling Mk 4 was also the basis of the Rebel Alliance's DH-17 blaster pistol, which featured in the original trilogy of Star Wars films and also *The Force Awakens* (2015) and *Rogue One* (2016). The legacy of the E-11 continues throughout the rest of the franchise, with the latest films featuring a blaster heavily influenced by the E-11. It is worth noting that throughout the films the Imperial stormtroopers never deploy their blasters' stocks; perhaps this accounts for their legendary inaccuracy.

More recently the Sterling has featured in films set during the 1960s and 1970s, including *The Last King of Scotland* (2007) and *The Man from U.N.C.L.E.* (2015). Sterlings have also appeared on the small screen in cult British television series such as *Doctor Who*, *The Professionals* and *Father Ted*. The Sterling has percolated into popular consciousness, arming charismatic spies and stormtroopers alike; its screen legacy will undoubtedly continue for years to come.

contacted the Sterling Armament Company to enquire how much a licence to produce Sterling's magazines would cost and was quoted an exorbitant fee. The Australian Government, unwilling to pay for the licence, produced them anyway. Sterling could not afford to take legal action to stop them. Instead, Sterling's new managing director, James Edmiston, eventually came to an informal agreement with the Australians. He agreed that they could produce the Sterling's magazine unlicensed as long as they did not sell them commercially – this would have eaten into Sterling's income. As previously discussed, the Australian Government purchased a total of 88 Sterling-Patchett Mk 5s which saw extensive use during operations in Vietnam.

The F1 was produced by the Lithgow Small Arms Factory in Lithgow, New South Wales, where as many as 25,000 were produced for the Australian military between 1963 and 1972. The F1s saw service in Vietnam, being issued to rear-echelon troops, armoured personnel carrier and aircraft crews and to infantry sections. It remained in service, alongside the L1A1, into the early 1990s when both were phased out of use as the 5.56×45mm F88 (Steyr AUG) was adopted.

CONCLUSION

George Patchett's submachine gun is a testament to its designer's ingenuity, skill and perseverance. With its excellent magazine, his weapon is widely regarded as one of the finest battle-tested submachine guns of its era. Its influence on its contemporaries is clear from the numerous clones and copies of its robust, reliable design. It also enjoys worldwide fame as the basis for the E-11 blaster rifle from the Star Wars film franchise.

While the role of the submachine gun was progressively subverted by the intermediate-calibre assault rifle after 1945, the weapon has survived in an increasingly niche role. Though the Sterling lacked the ease of modularity to take on the role of a modern special-forces weapon when compared to contemporaries such as the Heckler & Koch MP5, it continued to arm British troops until both it and the L1A1 self-loading rifle were finally replaced by the SA80, developed by the design team at RSAF Enfield. The last Sterlings were withdrawn from British service in 1994; while the Sterling was generally replaced by the SA80 as a personal defence weapon for front-line troops, it was not until the adoption of the L22A2 in 2003 that the SA80 series adequately filled the Sterling's role for aircraft and vehicle crews.

Facing tough competition from other firearms manufacturers, the Sterling Armament Company found that its sales slowed from the late 1970s. Certainly, by the 1980s Sterling's manufacturing system was increasingly dated; the ill-fated S11 project had highlighted the potential cost of retooling and updating the company's production line. In October 1983, James Edmiston sold Sterling and by January 1985, the company had entered liquidation. Sterling's assets were sold off before it was finally bought by Royal Ordnance, a subsidiary of British Aerospace Plc, and closed down in 1988. With the exception of a few specialized manufacturers like the precision rifle maker Accuracy International, the closure of the Sterling Armament Company saw the end of large-scale private manufacture of small arms in Britain. The Sterling submachine gun represents Britain's last commercially successful, widely purchased small arm.

These three Sterlings represent British-, Indian- and Canadian-produced versions of George Patchett's submachine gun. From left to right: British L2A2, Indian 1A1, Canadian C1. It is with Indian forces that the Sterling has seen its longest service; the SAF carbine continues to be used by the Indian Navy, Air Force and Army and most national and local police forces. (© Royal Armouries PR.1413, PR.9192 and PR.7598)

BIBLIOGRAPHY

Books

Arthur, Max (1985). *Above All, Courage: Personal Stories from the Falklands War*. London: Cassell.

Arthur, Max (1987). *Northern Ireland: Soldiers Talking*. London: Sidgwick & Jackson.

Bishop, Chris (2002). *Firepower: Infantry Weapons: Tactical Illustrations, Performance Specifications, First-hand Mission Reports*. London: Grange Books.

Bound, Graham (2007). *Invasion 1982: The Falkland Islanders' Story*. Barnsley: Pen & Sword.

Chanin, Eileen (2014). *Limbang Rebellion: Seven Days in December 1962*. Barnsley: Pen & Sword.

Cole, Pauline (2015). *Army Girl: the Untold Story*. Self-published.

Edmiston, James (2011). *The Sterling Years*. Barnsley: Pen & Sword.

Edmiston, James & Kormornick, Lawrence (2012). *The Sterling Redemption: Twenty-Five Years To Clear My Name*. Barnsley: Pen & Sword.

Fitz-Gibbon, Spencer (2001). *Not Mentioned in Despatches: The History and Mythology of the Battle of Goose Green*. Cambridge: James Clarke & Co. Ltd.

Franklin, Derek (1997). *A Pied Cloak: Memoirs of a Colonial Police (Special Branch) Officer*. London: Janus Publishing Co.

Helebrant, Martin (2016). *The Schmeisser Myth: German Submachine Guns Through Two World Wars*. Cobourg: Collector Grade Publications.

Hewitt, Peter (2008). *Kenya Cowboy: A Police Officer's Account of the Mau Mau Emergency*. Johannesburg: 30 Degrees South Publishers.

Laidler, Peter & Howroyd, David (1996). *Guns of Dagenham: Lanchester, Patchett, Sterling*. Cobourg: Collector Grade Publications.

Patchett, George (1948). *Patchett Machine Carbine Handbook*. Dagenham: Sterling Engineering Company Ltd.

Sterling Armament Company Limited (1974). *Sterling Patchett Silenced Sub-Machine gun, User Handbook, 9mm MK5/L34A1*. Dagenham: Sterling Armament Company Ltd.

van der Bijl, Nicholas (2017). *Mau Mau Rebellion: The Emergency in Kenya 1952–1956*. Barnsley: Pen & Sword.

Walker, Jonathan (2011). *Aden Insurgency: The Savage War in Yemen 1962–67*. Barnsley: Pen & Sword.

Wardman, Wayne (1991). *The Owen Gun*. Self-published.

Other sources

<http://www.parachuteregiment-hsf.org/Personal%20account.html>, accessed 29 August 2017.

<https://www.awm.gov.au/unit/U53506/>, accessed 20 May 2017.

Boss, Bill. 'More Details Released on New Machine-Carbine', in *Ottawa Citizen*, 15 June 1953.

'Record Attempts with Supercharged Twin', in *The Motor Cycle*, 11 March 1926.

'Extensive Record Breaking', in *The Motor Cycle*, 7 October 1926.

'Pendine!', in *The Motor Cycle*, 4 August 1927.

London Gazette

<https://www.thegazette.co.uk/London/issue/40413/supplement/1094>, accessed 28 May 2017.

<https://www.thegazette.co.uk/London/issue/43689/supplement/5969>, accessed 23 June 2017.

Sterling attempted to break into the US commercial and law-enforcement markets. Here, two officers from the Los Angeles Police Department pose with a Mk 4 (left) and a Mk 5 (right). (Courtesy of the Royal Armouries)

<https://www.thegazette.co.uk/London/issue/43691/page/5981>, accessed 12 July 2017.
<https://www.thegazette.co.uk/London/issue/47932/supplement/10661>, accessed 29 July 2017.
<https://www.thegazette.co.uk/London/issue/49134/supplement/12834>, accessed 28 July 2017.

Archive sources

Royal Armouries Library (Former MOD Pattern Room Library)
510(200) STER: Box 1, Box 2, Box 3.
240 Suppressed Weapons: Box 2.
Interviews conducted by the Imperial War Museum
<http://www.iwm.org.uk/collections/item/object/80012440>, accessed 4 August 2017.
<http://www.iwm.org.uk/collections/item/object/80023165>, accessed 10 July 2017.
<http://www.iwm.org.uk/collections/item/object/80023605>, accessed 28 August 2017.
<http://www.iwm.org.uk/collections/item/object/80023609>, accessed 25 June 2017.
<http://www.iwm.org.uk/collections/item/object/80024316>, accessed 25 July 2017.
<http://www.iwm.org.uk/collections/item/object/80024847>, accessed 28 August 2017.
<http://www.iwm.org.uk/collections/item/object/80025432>, accessed 30 May 2017.
<http://www.iwm.org.uk/collections/item/object/80026268>, accessed 30 June 2017.
<http://www.iwm.org.uk/collections/item/object/80031571>, accessed 16 August 2017.
National Archives
'Manufacture of sub-machine gun L2A3, Sterling Engineering Co Ltd and G W Patchett, claim against the Crown under section 46 of the Patents Act 1949' (1957–62) <http://discovery. nationalarchives.gov.uk/details/r/C3187292>, accessed 9 May 2018.
'Dispute as to Royalties on use of Patent for Carbine Gun' (1963–69) <http://discovery. nationalarchives.gov.uk/details/r/C63703>, accessed 9 May 2018.

INDEX

Figures in **bold** refer to illustrations.